How to
Survive and
Grow Richer
in the
Tough Times
Ahead

Also by Thomas J. Holt:

Total Investing

How to Survive and Grow Richer in the Tough Times Ahead

Thomas J. Holt

Rawson, Wade Publishers, Inc.
New York

LIBRARY OF CONGRESS CATALOGING IN PUBLICATION DATA
Holt, Thomas J   1928–
    How to survive and grow richer in the tough
times ahead.
        Includes index.
        1. Investments—Handbooks, manuals, etc.   I. Title.
HG4921.H64   332.6′78   80-5983
ISBN 0-89256-157-2

Published simultaneously in Canada by McClelland and
Stewart, Ltd.
Manufactured in the United States of America
Composition by American–Stratford Graphic Services,
Brattleboro, Vermont
Printed and bound by Fairfield Graphics,
Fairfield, Pennsylvania

Charts by Mary Kokoletsos
Designed by Gene Siegel
Fourth Printing October 1981

To My Wife Debbie and My Daughter Evelyn

Contents

Introduction

Long ago I discovered that opportunity doesn't knock only once. It keeps knocking. Only when you stop listening and learning do you stop hearing it.

And I discovered something else. You don't have to start with a large inheritance from a "rich uncle" to achieve financial well-being. If you make it a habit to put some money aside from your current income, and let that money work for you intelligently, you can build up a good-sized nest egg in good times or bad.

Nor do you need inside information, superior intelligence, and extraordinary good luck to invest successfully. These so-called "requirements" have all been greatly overrated. Time and time again, any number of independent thinking individuals have shown better investment results than corporate insiders and Wall Street experts.

In all frankness, these revelations didn't come to me overnight. I, too, had gone looking for surefire strategies and foolproof systems. And there certainly was no shortage of such schemes being offered to the novice. But no matter how promising they appeared at first, they invariably came a cropper in real application.

During the searching period, however, I acquired a

new understanding of the investment process itself, and a renewed respect for historical enlightenment. With their assistance, an *approach to intelligent investing* gradually emerged. And that approach has since been successfully proven in both bull and bear markets.

I emphasized the phrase "approach to intelligent investing"—because that's what this book is all about. There won't be any get-rich-quick formula or technique here. Rather, I'll try to show you what kind of investment climate you can expect for the 1980s and why, and how you can take advantage of it to enhance your capital growth without excessive risk.

The Workload Side of Monetary Magic

Those who manage to prosper even when most other people are losing their shirts are always the subject of envy or mystery or gossip. Who hasn't heard the endless tales about such market-made multimillionaires as Will Durant, Jesse Livermore, Bernard Baruch, Joseph Kennedy, Sr., and various others? Who hasn't wondered how they pulled it off? And who hasn't yearned for that special combination of extremely expert knowledge and good luck they possessed?

Stop right there! The details of how these men succeeded have been recited in many easily available books. I won't attempt to recreate them here. But I think it's highly noteworthy that their legendary successes have certain basic elements in common.

On close inspection, for example, you'll find that all of them knew the value of doing their own homework. They relied not on the conventional wisdom, but on their own independent research or personal economic analysis. Yes, some of them did occasionally benefit from advance or "inside" information. But far more importantly, they always made it their business to *know* what the market was doing, how the main money flow was moving, and when to take a new or minority position.

Of course, they didn't really always know. Every one of them was "wrong" at one time or another, and the penalties they paid ranged from massive financial losses to national notoriety and public ridicule. At those times, Lady Luck seemed to have abandoned them altogether—if indeed she had ever been a factor in making their fortunes.

But somehow, they all soon reemerged to become the legendary financiers that we now know so well.

How did they do it? By persevering and being willing to keep on learning, especially from their own mistakes. These are qualities that have always received a great deal of lip service, but which few investors actually put into practice. Not many are willing to pay the price.

And what is that "price"? Sheer hard work: like maintaining surveillance over the full spectrum of investment securities; like learning to make your own judgments instead of following the crowd; like studying the investment practices and economic problems of earlier generations.

Hard work, yes. But certainly not beyond the capabilities of most private investors. As this book progresses, I'll pinpoint the key principles of successful investment management for you. I also intend to strip away any mystery or apprehensions you may feel about accepting, if not making, long-term economic forecasts. And if the investment psychology of the 1970s is still fresh in your mind, I'll even show you how and why it should be discarded and replaced by a totally new way of thinking.

By the time you finish reading this book, I'm convinced, you'll agree that successful investing doesn't have to be enjoyed by somebody else. It is there for you to go after.

November 1980   Thomas J. Holt

It's Always a Good Time to Make Money

CHAPTER ONE

Investment Opportunities in This Century

Back in my high school days, I didn't care much for history. Like any wide-eyed youngster, I then thought, "Why bother with living in the past? There's a brand new, totally different future just ahead. And that's the world I'll be living in."

In all fairness to myself, though, I must say that my history teachers then didn't help matters much. They usually insisted that we students memorize hundreds of names and dates, most of which I have since found to be of little significance. Besides, I always hated straight memorization. It doesn't give me a chance to think things out logically.

But in college, I had a history professor who followed quite a different teaching approach. Instead of putting heavy emphasis on pinpointing which general captured which town on which date, he concentrated mainly on discussing why certain historical developments took place, and how they directly or indirectly affected future events. Every one of his classes was like a storytelling session. And from attending his lectures, I began to appreciate the importance of knowing history. I found that the answers to many of our present and future problems very often lie in the past.

History, of course, does not pertain only to social and political evolution. It encompasses economic developments, as well. As a matter of fact, almost all social and political upheavals of the past were somehow linked to economic considerations. And economic changes, of course, have a lot to do with changing investment opportunities.

Unfortunately, few investors bother to study the history of economics and finance. And in some cases, where people belatedly learn about other people's recent investment successes, the "knowledge" often turns out to be a liability. Assuming that what has been successful for others in the recent past will remain successful for themselves in the future, these Johnnies-come-lately often end up paying dearly for making the very same investment mistakes their predecessors made.

This is not to say that we should expect past economic and financial developments to be duplicated in the future. Not at all. In fact, I have yet to find two historical periods that are truly identical. However, the investor who takes a little time to study history will soon discover that successful investing is not an impossible dream. There are systematic ways to determine where good opportunities lie.

Similarly, the history-studying investor will find that no investment vehicle remains attractive indefinitely. Sometimes, for example, stocks are a good buy; but sometimes they definitely are not. And I'm not talking about weeks or months, but years in which equities are either promising or just pure poison. So, when stocks are in an underlying uptrend, by all means invest in them. But as times change, the investor must start looking for new money-making opportunities. Holding on to obsolete investment strategies and vehicles is nothing less than throwing good money after bad.

Keep in mind, too, that the investigative investor who examines history will pass through a series of widely disparate economic eras in which roaring booms and protracted depressions were recorded. Invariably, this journey will show that successful investment performances were sustained by many people under all types of economic conditions. These were the investors who remained open-minded, flexible, and willing to work at attaining realistic goals. They refused to indulge in wishful thinking or to submit to fear and despair. They combined self-discipline with common sense, logic, and investment know-how. And whatever happened, they achieved financial success.

In my opinion, almost anyone with reasonable intelligence can master these basic skills. And many more of us should make the effort. It doesn't require expert knowledge. What's vital, of course, is to gain a good understanding of the current and prospective investment climate, and the methods by which to benefit from this knowledge.

As a beginning step to acquiring sound investment skills, then, let's look at some of the areas in which Americans, without exposing themselves to excessive risks, were able to achieve good investment results in the past. This short trip into yesteryear can go a long way toward understanding why different investment opportunities emerged in various periods and what we can reasonably expect for the years ahead.

Actually, we don't have to go too far back. Until the twentieth century began, most Americans regarded investing as merely putting money in the banks and collecting interest. The securities markets of those days were the playground for a select few, and the commodities market was used mainly by farmers. Those Americans who didn't depend on wages as their sole income were engaged mostly in farming and small businesses.

In the early 1900s, however, Americans finally began to have some liquid savings to invest in a meaningful way. This was also the period when the building of great corporate wealth started to gather momentum. Even so, less than 1% of the population could then be described as investors. But because the U.S. population was so large, compared to most other industrialized countries, they represented a group substantial enough to create a viable investment market for that era.

As it turned out, the first decade of this century was a good period for equity investment. To be sure, there was the so-called "rich man's panic" in 1903–1904 and another bear market in 1907–1908 which was caused by an economic depression. Still, for the investor who was willing and able to stay put and ride with the underlying upward trend, the reward was good. Between 1900 and the start of 1910, the Dow Jones Industrial Average rose nearly 50%.

The ensuing decade, which encompassed World War I, didn't offer very much to the long-term investor. The market underwent many wide swings, to be sure. But between 1910 and 1920, the Dow Jones industrials actually show a net decline.

And bonds did not do any better during that same period. As measured by the High-Grade Corporate Bond Index compiled by Standard & Poor's, they also declined more than 10% between 1910 and 1920.

Nonetheless, there were other good investment opportunities around. Real estate in general and private homes in particular were then in the midst of a strong bull market of their own. Specifically, the median sales price of new homes rose from about $4,300 in 1905 to $7,800 in 1925. That twenty-year gain was equivalent to a solid 81%.

After a bad start in its first year, the 1920s, by and large, belonged to the stock market. As the Roaring Twenties moved toward their peak in late 1929, the number of investors interested in stocks and their attitude toward stocks both changed markedly. These investors were convinced they couldn't do anything wrong, and until the big crash in late 1929, the substantial profits being generated by stocks proved they were right.

Specifically, the decade started with the Dow Jones Industrial Average standing just a shade below 100. At the 1929 peak, by contrast, it was around 370.

The 1929 crash started a sharp decline for stock prices, of course. It was also accompanied by major declines in commodities and real estate properties as well. Thus, the next decade, with its tragic Great Depression, was decidedly unprofitable for the average holder of stocks and other investment properties. But even so, substantial monies were still being made by many people during that period.

For one thing, when the stock market hit bottom in 1932, those who had the courage and the money to buy were able to make a fortune speedily. Note, however, that in order to take advantage of the bargains available in depressed markets, the successful investor must have adequate buying power when the bargains become available. And that was a tall order in 1932, considering the erupting financial crisis that led to widespread bank closings in the following year.

Still, the 1930s was full of low-risk investment opportunities. And they were most readily available in the fixed-income bond market. In fact, in that very worst decade in U.S. economic history, the average bond appreciated nearly 25%.

During the World War II years, bond prices continued to climb. But they weren't really exciting investments. For instance, the Standard & Poor's Composite Index rose from 1940 to 1946, when it peaked, by only 6%. That's equivalent to less than 1% a year compounded. Reflecting the government's easy-money policy, meanwhile, bond yields over the same period were as low as 3%.

By contrast, common stocks once again became a very desirable investment vehicle. They started a long-term upward trend in 1942, and throughout the 1940s most blue chip stocks yielded 10% or more.

Ironically, not many people bought stocks during those years. Memories of the 1929 crash were still strong. Investors by and large shied away from the equity market. On top of that, many also feared that a postwar depression, as happened after World War I, was inevitable.

But some investors did increasingly accumulate common stocks throughout the 1940s. Toward the end of that decade, their accumulation was substantial enough to effect a new rise in stock prices. As a result, the decade of the 1950s started with the Dow Jones Industrial Average just about double what it had been a decade earlier.

Stocks continued to represent a highly favorable and gratifying investment vehicle throughout the 1950s and 1960s. By 1968, the Dow industrials were around 1,000, or 600% higher than back in 1950. At that point, the stock market was conspicuously different in nature from that prevailing two decades earlier.

Specifically, investors in the late 1940s and early 1950s were mostly careful stock buyers nibbling at bargains gingerly. Most of them put away their purchases for long-term growth. There was little churning of investment portfolios. Thus, trading on the New York Stock Exchange averaged less than two million shares a day.

In the late 1960s, by way of contrast, the market was dominated by in-and-out traders anxious to make a fast profit. And this group by no means consisted of only private speculators. Most managers supervising large pension funds and other trusts also fell into that category. Market turnover was intense. On the New York Stock Exchange, the daily trading volume averaged well over 30 million shares.

As it turned out, the late 1960s also marked the end of the long-term bull market. In the ensuing ten years, the Dow Jones industrials never managed to stay above 1,000 very long. At the end of the decade, in fact, the Dow stood at 850, or actually lower than the level prevailing in the late 1960s.

But the 1970s also saw the nation's inflation rate accelerated. As most Americans became painfully aware, ever-rising prices caused the dollar to lose its purchasing power rapidly. To be specific, the Dow Jones Industrial Average, adjusted for the rise in consumer prices, actually declined more than 60% in the 1970s!

Adding insult to injury, common stocks also provided unacceptably low dividend returns to shareholders. Over the decade, for example, the average yield of the stocks comprising the DJIA was only 4%. Bonds, on the other hand, yielded on average around 6%.

Nevertheless, long-term bonds were no bargain in the 1970s either. While their yields were higher than stocks, their prices performed no better than stocks. The Standard & Poor's Bond Index started the 1970s at 68.63 and ended that decade at 51.09.

The fact that stocks and bonds were unsatisfactory investments, however, didn't mean that no one was able to achieve capital growth in the 1970s. As a matter of fact, many were again willing to buck the general trend and search for new investment outlets overlooked by the majority. Among the areas in which many investors did extremely well were real estate and precious metals.

Prior to the 1970s, home buying was routinely undertaken only by those who wanted to be homeowners. But because demand kept increasing, prices of homes generally

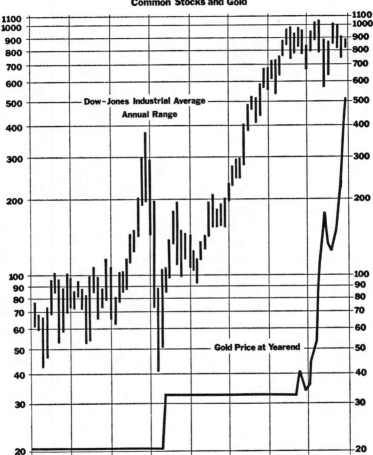

Common Stocks and Gold

The postwar bull market ended in the late 1960s. In the decade of the 1970s stock prices moved sideways. In non-inflated dollars, in fact, the Dow Jones Industrial Average actually lost more than 60%. By contrast, gold was an excellent investment; it skyrocketed far more than enough to compensate for inflation.

trended upward. By the early 1970s, the continuing uptrend of home prices was attracting even those investors who would not otherwise be interested in homeownership. Demand began rising at an exponential rate. So did prices. Result: the median sales price of new one-family homes rose from around $25,000 at the start of the decade to over $63,000 at the end.

Precious metals did even better. Actually, at the start of the 1970s Americans weren't legally allowed to buy or own gold. But then, not many Americans were interested anyway. The Establishment often bad-mouthed the metal, calling it a "barbarous relic." Many so-called "experts" also insisted that had gold not been supported by the U.S. government at $35 an ounce for many years, it might not even command a market price of as much as $5 an ounce!

As usual, some investors had enough foresight to depart from the conventional wisdom. Before gold buying was legalized, they acquired gold coins and stocks of gold mining companies. And once ownership was legalized in 1974, they started accumulating bullion as well. At any rate, the price of gold skyrocketed in the 1970s, starting from the official $35 an ounce rate in 1971 and rising to $850 and higher in January 1980.

Numerous other examples could be cited. But the above review has made it quite clear, I hope, that at any given time there are always some investment vehicles enjoying an uptrend. And it's at these times that investors can enjoy capital growth without exposing themselves to excessive risks.

The thing to remember, though, is that any uptrend in any investment vehicle typically starts with few investors showing any interest. To enjoy bargains, therefore, the astute investor must be willing to take a minority position, even if it means being ridiculed by friends and relatives.

As the uptrend unfolds, the need to fight the consensus

of skeptics will lessen. That's because more and more investors will have recognized the wisdom of buying the investment vehicle in question. And as the uptrend accelerates, so will the purchase or selling price. This is the simple result of supply-demand forces in any marketplace.

Toward the end of the uptrend, however, the astute investor must once again be willing to assume a minority position. For at this juncture, the market is inevitably dominated by excessive speculation. Instead of trying to pick off the very top dollar, the astute investor should now begin taking profits while the going is good—and turn his or her attention to other investment opportunities.

My emphasis on this kind of commonsense approach to investing has evolved over many years. It was first defined in a book titled *Total Investing*, which I wrote in the mid-1970s. If anything, the key elements of this concept are even more essential for successful investing today:

1. Be willing and able to analyze economic and market development independently.

2. Be prepared to adjust investment strategies quickly as economic and market conditions change, shifting portfolio composition to reduce risk exposure, as well as to take advantage of free-market forces.

3. Be open-minded enough to recognize and make use of investment opportunities offered by securities and techniques other than buying stocks.

4. Be ready to take a minority position steadfastly, whenever necessary.

It's as simple as that. Each point is predicated on developments of the past eight decades. Each is brief, easily remembered, and supportive of the others. Together they are applicable to any kind of economic climate. So ask yourself this question: Doesn't it make pure common sense to base your investment strategy on these four principles?

CHAPTER TWO

The Economic Ups and Downs

We have seen in the last chapter that for one reason or another, investing in stocks was highly rewarding in certain periods, but terribly disappointing in others. The same held true for bonds, precious metals, and other investment vehicles.

At this point, however, it must be emphasized that in discussing favorable or unfavorable periods, I was referring primarily to the main underlying trend. Within every such major trend, there are inevitably any number of counter-moves of substantial magnitude and longevity. Moreover, even when the broad market is advancing, there are always numerous delinquent issues that go down.

The equity market of the 1970s is an appropriate case in point. For the decade as a whole, the popular averages showed no net gain at all. Yet, during those ten years, the market underwent quite a number of wide swings. For veteran investors, it was very worthwhile to take advantage of those interim movements. Moreover, many individual stocks and stock groups fluctuated even more erratically than the averages—so much so that nimble in-and-out

13

traders were actually able to multiply their capital many-fold.

But the key words above are "veteran investors" and "nimble traders." The fact is, capitalizing successfully on secondary or isolated movements is something easier said than done by the lay investor. Unless you keep abreast of economic and financial developments and prospects regularly—or unless you have professional help—playing the market, as distinguished from investing for the long pull, will more likely than not make only your broker rich.

Moreover, it is a fact that the interim movements of many individual stocks are frequently generated, if not manipulated, by Wall Street professionals. The odds are, therefore, stacked very much against you, the outsider. Those issues which are easily glamorized or promoted by a "good story"—and which have a small floating supply and hence a relatively thin market—are especially vulnerable to being moved up or down artificially.

How are stocks "moved" artificially? It usually begins when wealthy financiers first pinpoint an issue that seems reasonably cheap by one measure or another, but is not in any way popular. They start to quietly accumulate large chunks of that stock. They then let the Wall Street community get in on the "second floor" by introducing the stock to brokers and securities analysts. The latter then get the public excited with bullish buy recommendations. Simultaneously, the sponsors undertake some sort of public relations program to glorify the company and its progress. Once demand from the unsuspecting public is so stimulated, the stock takes off on heavy trading volume.

Even as the public gets all excited, however, insiders unload their holdings and take their profits. The late-arriving traders soon find themselves stuck with an over-priced stock in a thin market with very few buyers around.

Even blue chip issues are not immune to such artificial

influences. It is estimated, for instance, that at the start of this decade, the five largest investment management organizations alone controlled some $84 billion of pension fund and other tax-exempt assets. And the top 100 money managers combined control $367.5 billion of such funds. As a result of this extreme concentration, any money manager can single-handedly drive up the price of a given stock or stocks for weeks, and sometimes even months. And many have indeed done just that.

Ironically, neither the investing public nor the trusts that are managed by these banks benefit from such artificial price bulges. Once the hyped buying binges are completed, the stocks involved more often than not drop back to their previous levels. As a result, the pension funds end up with a higher-than-necessary average cost for their acquisitions. And those outside investors who like to put their money "where the action is" again find themselves buying stocks near the peak of an artificial advance.

Some people, of course, do profit from these periodic drives. The real beneficiaries are insiders who capitalize on the money managers' actions and move in and out rapidly. True enough, the Securities and Exchange Commission has instituted strict rules forbidding insiders from realizing personal gains of this kind. But it would be naïve to believe that such hanky-panky isn't really widespread in the Wall Street jungle. To circumvent SEC rules, all the pros have to do is to trade in the accounts of friends or relatives or use secret accounts in foreign banks.

Notwithstanding the above, it remains perfectly safe for the lay investor to go with the major underlying trend. These are investment market movements that typically persist for many years, and are determined strictly by free-market forces. Occasionally, of course, these trends may be temporarily disturbed by big money operations. But, in the long run, free-market forces always prevail.

To capitalize on major market trends, however, one must first recognize what the underlying economic condition is or will soon become. This is not to say that a growing economy is always good for stocks or that a contracting economy must always be good for bonds. But there is no question whatsoever that the ups and downs of the economy do directly affect the supply and demand for all kinds of investment vehicles.

So let's again take a brief look at what happened in the earlier decades of this century. In Chapter 1, you'll recall, it was pointed out that the first decade was a good period for equity investment, while the second decade didn't offer very much to long-term securities investors. Now let's see how the economy behaved during those periods.

Looking at the record between 1900 and 1910, we see that the GNP (in current dollars) rose from $19.4 billion to $35.4 billion, an increase of over 82%. The growth rate was almost three times that of the previous decade. Even more important, there was nothing at all comparable to the destructive inflation rates and overwhelming debt loads that stifled recent economic growth. In fact, numerous industries were in hyperactive growth stages, and the building of great corporate wealth was exemplified by U.S. Steel, which had become America's first billion-dollar corporation.

It was during this period, moreover, that the U.S. became a world power—both militarily and in foreign trade. Soon after the Spanish-American War ended, the economic development of a so-called "American empire" had spread out from Alaska to Hawaii to the Philippines to Puerto Rico and, for a time, to Cuba. U.S. profits from such business investments have been enormous ever since.

In addition, most of the key economic indicators were then conducive to big business growth. Corporate profits shot up year after year. Productivity rates also climbed continuously. Prices and wages were stable or falling at times, but annual unemployment rates usually remained low, while business investments usually rose higher and higher.

Under this very favorable combination of circumstances, the investment markets flourished and investors generally did very well. For those with money to invest, it was a good case of being in the right place at the right time.

The following decade, however, was a much different story. Once again, the annual GNP continued rising at then unprecedented rates. In current dollars, it jumped close to 160%—from $35.4 billion in 1910 to $91.5 billion in 1920. But most of it was accounted for by inflation. Adjusted for price increases, the real GNP showed surprisingly little net gain. In terms of the 1972 dollar, it merely grew from $186 billion in 1910 to $213 billion in 1920, an increase for the entire ten-year period of less than 15%.

To be sure, there were many favorable economic developments within the second decade. Urbanization and industrialization were replacing agriculture and westward migration as the major forces in the U.S. economy. Prior to 1910, more than 60% of the U.S. population had lived on farms or in small towns. But as railroads expanded greatly and more highways appeared, people became increasingly mobile. The end result was the explosive growth of large American cities, vast industrial expansion, and the abrupt decline of traditional frontier/agricultural lifestyles.

What's more, there was a gradual dispersal of the longtime concentration of financial power in the big northeastern states. As more cities and more industries prospered and grew, new investment centers and major banks mushroomed across the nation, too. For the first time, the big money ventures were being put together as frequently in Detroit, Chicago, Denver, San Francisco, etc., as they previously had been in New York or Boston or Philadelphia.

None of these trends, however, can conceal the decade's basic underlying sluggishness. From 1910 through 1912, overall growth was moderate, but hardly satisfactory in any sense. Then, in 1913, came rumors of U.S. entry into World War I. Business became panicky. Commodity prices plunged downward. Unemployment rose sharply, and many corporate failures occurred. The GNP barely exceeded that of the previous year.

The panic continued until war was finally declared in August 1914, and then immediately worsened. At that time, the stock exchanges actually closed down for more than three months. For the whole year, the GNP plunged well below the 1912–13 level.

The recovery in 1915 was surprisingly swift. It began as wartime orders poured in from Europe. U.S. financing of the war also spurred industrial production. Incidentally, it wasn't noticed then, but Liberty Bond campaigns being conducted by the U.S. government helped greatly to educate the general public about the intricacies of profitable investment practices.

Along with a return to more prosperous times, however, the war-directed economy also induced a substantial rate of inflation. From mid-1915 through 1918, inflation soared progressively higher. The economy benefited, of course, from heavy wartime expenditures. But many of these gains were quickly offset by rising prices in an era when wage levels hardly rose at all.

For two years (1919–20) after World War I, inflation maintained a false order of prosperity in the U.S. The GNP was rising in current dollars, but when adjusted for inflation, the net loss was very substantial indeed. Many manufacturers and retailers were depressed by high wartime inventories they couldn't sell at home. Commodity prices again fell sharply, and then stocks declined as well.

Let's pause now and see what history teaches us as far as correlation between investment opportunities and economic development is concerned.

For starters, it confirms what most people believe—a long period of solid economic growth is conducive to a rising stock market. It generates a hefty supply of new investment capital, and more important, it creates the desire on the part of the investing public to participate in the national growth via equity ownership; hence, the general market's uptrend between 1900 and 1910.

Actually, common stocks did suffer a couple of sinking spells during that decade. But they were preceded and then followed by strong advances, so that the market's underlying advance remained intact. Those interim swings were caused mainly by the flow of speculative monies into and out of the market. As I mentioned earlier, long-term investors are better off not trying to catch such interim moves.

But the history of the first two decades also taught us another important lesson—a lesson many investors had to learn the hard way in the 1970s. To wit: rapid inflation is not compatible with a rising stock market. Between 1910 and 1920, the GNP managed to surge upward, but almost all the gain was accounted for by inflation. During that decade, as a result, stock prices showed hardly any net gain in current dollars and a big loss in inflation-adjusted dollars. Bonds also did poorly for the same reason. But real estate, being a good inflation hedge, enjoyed strong price increases.

Now, let's proceed to the 1920s. In the wake of World War I, a deep depression unfolded. The wartime boom had been unreal, so business faltered as soon as military spending slowed.

Fortunately, the U.S. export trades soon started booming. Europe was recovering from a badly war-torn economy. It was cash poor to be sure, but to sustain this vital overseas trade, the U.S. government made numerous loans to wartime allies. Even when their monetary systems collapsed, as some did, still more loans were made so Europe could continue buying American goods with American money.

In certain respects, looking back, the 1910–20 period had its pluses. In those ten years, the total capital of Big Business rose tremendously. The diversity and production capabilities of U.S. industry outdistanced those of any other nation. The curtain was rising, in effect, on an era of high investment activity and capital growth such as the world had never seen.

Leading the way in this remarkable onward-upward growth surge was the automotive industry. Annual new car production skyrocketed from about 10,000 to over 2 million vehicles as the decade ended. No other innovation, before or since, has provided as dynamic a stimulus to national investment fever or total industrial growth as did the automobile.

And the Big Business bandwagon didn't stop after reaching Detroit. The auto boom created enormous growth in other major industries: oil, steel, rubber, road building, even tourism; all this plus countless parts-and-services suppliers for original equipment and the ubiquitous automotive after-market.

Meanwhile, the availability and rapid growth of electric power was stimulating development of still other spin-off industries, among which were household lighting equipment, appliances, power-driven machinery, movies, and radio. With each such industrial development, of course, the bond and equity markets were tapped for heavy financing—and investors were deluged with an ever-growing variety of new issues to consider.

It was in this kind of vigorously fluctuating economic environment that the impetus was created for the next decade to become known as the Roaring Twenties. By then, it seemed, growth and more growth was all that mattered. Except for the sharp postwar drop in 1921, the economy expanded steadily and substantially. Despite a slowdown in growth rate in the final years, for instance, the GNP exceeded the $100 billion level in 1929 for the first time. In current dollars, it represented a more than fivefold increase over the 1900 mark, and was almost three times greater than that in 1910.

Gradually and steadily, personal savings also moved upward. And although the real wealth then being generated was quite considerable in itself, don't forget that it was further blessed by very low corporate and personal income taxes.

While 1929 is remembered as the end of the Roaring Twenties, the turning point actually came as early as 1927–28. For some years prior, there was an intense ballyhoo about America's invincible financial vigor. The consensus of politicians, bankers, and economists seemed undeniably true, and it boiled down to this: "Nothing can arrest the upward movement."

Small investors and large, veterans and neophytes, all accepted the conventional wisdom without any questions. In fact, the volume of trading in common stocks increased more in the 1920s than it ever has in any single decade. But it was too good to last. In the fall of 1929 came the big crash. For most investors, dreams of overnight profits turned into the nightmare of instant bankruptcies.

In retrospect, most economists today still can't agree on what went wrong and why. Quite clearly, however, many warning signals that had appeared long before the crash occurred were ignored. Here are some of them:

• Business investments began declining. They dropped from almost $17 billion in 1926 to $15 billion in 1928, before starting to recover.

• The bull market of 1928–29 disguised a severe housing depression which had started in 1927. It also encouraged many manufacturers to build excess capacity, or burdensome inventories, or both.

• After rising steadily throughout the decade, the M1 money supply (currency and demand deposits) leveled off in 1928. Failure of the Federal Reserve Board to restimulate this growth is still blamed by some economists for triggering the 1929 disaster and prolonging the Great Depression which followed.

In short, then, while the advance in stock prices during the greater part of that decade was spurred by solid economic growth, its continuation in the late 1920s was attributed almost entirely to unwarranted projection of economic growth into the distant future. And the lesson to be learned from history here is that stocks do often climb in the absence of real economic progress. But a bull market that ignores unfavorable realities can never be sustained. The longer and stronger such a rise takes place, the harder the subsequent fall must be.

Early efforts (1929–32) of the federal government to revive the stock market and speed economic recovery were entirely ineffectual. (The Dow Jones Industrial Average lost nearly 90% of its value during those years.) This was a role in which Washington then had relatively little experience, and one it was not yet ready to accept.

But the times were ripe for far-reaching changes. Seizing the opportunity, critics of the free enterprise system derided the claim that "that government is best which governs least." Big Business was floundering helplessly, they noted, and laissez-faire capitalism, which began in Civil War days, was no longer providing the corrections it had in the past.

To the shell-shocked public, these charges seemed reasonable. During the so-called Great Contraction period, from August 1929 through March 1933, the following events were recorded:

• Gross private domestic investments plunged from $16.2 billion to below $1 billion. The real GNP fell 30%, and industrial production alone nosedived 50%.

• As a result of a liquidity squeeze, deflation developed; prices fell 31% at wholesale and 25% at retail, while consumption spending declined 20%.

• Recurrent waves of panic swept through the banking system, forcing more than 9,000 banks to close their doors. More than 9 million savings accounts were lost, and many thousands of businesses went bankrupt.

• The unemployment rate reached 25% of the total labor force—up from 3.2% in 1929—and was still over 17% as late as 1939.

In terms of investor attitudes and economic activities of all kinds, the Great Depression was a tidal wave of total destruction. It altered forever the historic mystique of perpetual annual growth in which Americans have always taken such great pride. It made the federal government more active and dominant in economic affairs, while business became increasingly docile.

In short, like Humpty Dumpty, the renowned U.S. economic system had been fractured in so many places that putting it all together again seemed like an impossible task.

It wasn't impossible, of course. The records show that

the GNP began recovering in 1934. But, as later events have demonstrated, many of the "solutions" devised in Washington for ending the Great Depression eventually created even greater fiscal and economic problems than those that dominated the 1930s.

Specifically, interventionist government replaced laissez-faire with a bang in March 1933, after the inauguration of Franklin D. Roosevelt as president. Over the next three months, Congress passed some fifteen major bills to stimulate economic growth and restore national confidence. All in all, ninety-three pieces of legislation affecting banking, business, labor, agriculture, social welfare, and the various investment markets were passed during President Roosevelt's first two terms.

Out of this legislative whirlwind came a vast network of regulatory agencies and satellite bureaucracies. Most of them have survived the passing years, growing in power and scope and annual cost to taxpayers. Some of what they accomplished was necessary and desirable. At the same time, the cumulative effect of this creeping fiscal metamorphosis has been to create a national economy in which virtually all growth rates—and most investment opportuni ties—are either dictated or regulated or adjusted by federal agencies and federal policymakers.

It was the British economist, John Maynard Keynes, who first convinced FDR and many others in the U.S. to replace laissez-faire with federal programs financed by deficit spending. Under the Keynesian principles of *guided* capitalism, if nobody else is spending or buying, then the government must spend or buy. If business isn't hiring people and paying wages, then the government must create work and make wages possible. If the money supply isn't adequate for the nation's needs, and it wasn't in the 1930s, the government must print more and more money, and then devise new ways for pumping it into circulation.

In other words, the basic Keynesian strategy was to force-feed so much money into the economy that consumer buying power would be greatly increased. As this happened, industry—theoretically—would have new sales demands to supply and more jobs to fill, and the entire spectrum of business activity would accelerate. And so, since all other efforts had failed, the pump-priming programs in Washington began.

By 1937, the Keynesian concepts and the many welfare state activities advocated by President Roosevelt had been firmly established as federal fiscal policies. Together, they represented what was then called the New Deal. Deficit spending was no longer seen as just an emergency-relief device—it was here to stay. Washington had become, and still remains, one vast, interlocking transfer system for dispensing federal funds.

Throughout this period, however, none of the Keynesian fiscal strategies being attempted were effective enough to restore prosperity. The GNP's decline had bottomed in 1933 at $55.8 billion, and throughout the rest of the decade it remained far below the 1929 peak. In addition, more than 10 million people were still unemployed, and business growth ranged from sporadic to slow and sluggish. It wasn't until after World War II began that the Great Depression finally ended.

For investors, the fiasco of the 1930s provided a good lesson; to wit, when money gets extremely tight, a liquidity squeeze occurs. And when that happens, the acute need for cash typically causes many to liquidate both goods and investments involuntarily. As a result, prices tumble across the board; stocks and bonds are no exception. This, then, is the time to buy bargains. To be able to do so, though, the investor must first keep himself liquid with ample cash reserves.

Once the squeeze is over, money becomes progressively

cheaper. This is especially so if the government also follows an easy-money policy. The resulting drop in interest sends bond prices climbing. In such an environment, the bond market becomes the safest and softest place in which to build wealth.

Actually, even before Pearl Harbor, a recovery was beginning to take hold. As the U.S. once again aided its allies and prepared itself for war in the late 1930s, production soared in numerous basic industries, especially those related to the war effort. Agriculture also benefited greatly from increased demand abroad and rising prices at home. Thus, in 1940, the GNP again reached $100 billion, the magic level first topped in 1929. But the 1940 dollar was worth *more* than the 1929 dollar. On a unit basis, the 1940 GNP was some 10% higher.

World War II started in late 1941, and it helped accelerate the economic recovery. The armed forces draft absorbed thousands of young men who hadn't been able to find jobs. And high unemployment rates finally disappeared altogether. Over the next five years, the annual GNP growth more than doubled.

As it turned out, the war completed the recovery that Keynesian economics had barely been able to get started. Buoyant with massive government spending, the wartime years put money in people's pockets again. But they also created consumer demands for products and services which couldn't be satisfied—because of wartime priorities—until after the war.

As the war years wound down, Keynesian doctrines gradually became the basis of a new world economic order. This began at the famous Bretton Woods Conference of 1944 in New Hampshire, where the International Monetary Fund and the World Bank were created for financing postwar redevelopment programs. Both institutions soon brought Keynesian management techniques (government intervention, deficit spending, etc.) into the expansive economic programs of participating nations.

After the war, of course, the combination of advancing Communist power blocs and war-devastated economies was everywhere. Through the Marshall Plan, the Bretton Woods agreements, and other programs, the U.S. pumped out billions of dollars to rebuild Europe and Japan and to aid developing nations. For the next quarter century, the U.S. was at the center of free-world economic development. And the U.S. dollar ultimately became the universal reserve currency of central banks in most nations.

It is generally agreed, however, that the Full Employment Act of 1946 actually represented the greatest triumph of Keynesian economics within the U.S. This legislation required the president and Congress to promote maximum employment, production, and purchasing power through all available policy tools. It focused almost entirely on federal spending to stimulate the demand requirements of economic growth, leaving supply needs to free-market forces.

Helped in part by implementation of this act, but more by free-market forces, the next two decades—when inflation was negligible—produced the era of America's greatest economic growth. The GNP rose from $209.6 billion in 1946 to $420.7 billion in 1956 to $753 billion in 1966.

It was this solid economic growth, together with increasing investors' confidence, that sent common stock prices trending strongly upward. Between V-J Day and early 1966, the Dow Jones Industrial Average soared from about 170 to 1,000, a sixfold increase.

In contrast, bond prices, after peaking in 1946, have showed a long-term decline. They had moved consistently higher all through the Depression and World War II years. But since that time, even the most sophisticated investors have found that the performance of bond markets offers few big money-making opportunities.

In many respects, the 1950s and 1960s were similar to the early 1920s. America had again entered the world stage —on a vastly larger scale, to be sure—after concluding another costly war. Industrial production was booming, sparked by new growth industries and peacetime conversions of wartime technology. Enormous investments were being made in nuclear power, plastics, sophisticated communications systems, data processing, air travel, convenience foods, etc. And, of course, the born-again automotive industry was once more setting new growth records every year, while pulling numerous supplier industries along with it.

It needs to be noted, too, that the space age had arrived. America's race to reach the moon and other planets before Russia did was a major stimulant to the economy, as well as to national pride. Concurrently, conventional weaponry was being replaced with long-range missiles, nuclear submarines, jet aircraft, and elaborate early warning systems. The defense industries had never been so busy or productive in any peacetime era of U.S. history.

Between 1950 and 1970, total assets of all U.S. commercial banks rose from about $185 billion to over $500 billion. Other key indicators showed similar gains. And corporate profits moved generally upward. By 1969, when the bull market was climaxing, corporate equities were again as popular as they had been in 1929.

In effect, the end result of Keynesian economics in their peak years was to bring investors back to the very same point of see-no-evil where laissez-faire had crashed so harshly some forty years earlier.

But by then there was one big difference. In 1929, the Federal Reserve Board made some efforts to protect the dollar and restrict the money supply growth; in 1969, the

Board treated the dollar with "benign neglect" and prepared for a decade of rapid money supply growth.

In all fairness, the Fed itself cannot really create money. That occurs only when banking institutions lend money to borrowers by crediting their checking accounts. But Washington repeatedly made it easier and easier for banks to extend credit. Meanwhile, both the banking and business communities joined forces to promote the buy-now-pay-later habit. Result: the nation's money supply (M1B) skyrocketed at an average 8.9% annual rate in the 1970s, up sharply from the 5.0% average of the first twenty-five postwar years. The increase in the annual growth rate is equivalent to 78%!

What was the outcome? Only one word can be used to describe the 1970s accurately: *malaise.* The decade witnessed two severe recessions and, more devastatingly, rampant inflation.

Conventional wisdom was especially inept in its efforts to anticipate and measure the recurrent explosions of inflation. It certainly was not correct to single out OPEC's oil price hikes as the root cause, as many "experts" did. For in 1979, with the inflation rate averaging 13.3%, energy prices accounted for only a 3.5% increase. Even if stable energy costs had been maintained, inflation was already reaching double-digit levels and still climbing.

Traditional yardsticks always become increasingly unreliable as inflation takes hold. The annual GNP totals, for example, jumped nearly $1.5 trillion—from $982.4 billion in 1970 to $2.4 trillion in 1979, a seemingly enviable growth rate. Yet, when adjusted to 1972 dollars, the real GNP growth amounts to a moderate $356 billion for the entire decade.

Similar distortions were created by inflation in the growth indicators for virtually all key areas of the U.S. economy. As a result, the uncertainties facing investors to-

Gross National Product

$Bil.

One reason why stocks and bonds did poorly and the gold price soared in the 1970s was the accelerating inflation of that decade. Even as the gross national product expressed in current dollars accelerated, the nation's real economic growth slowed. Americans' confidence in the business prospect dropped to the lowest level since the Great Depression.

day have multiplied many times over. Through most of the 1970s, the stock market remained flat, and investor activity (as described in the previous chapter) was increasingly diversified among alternative vehicles.

Corporations and banks floundered around in the same boat. Both groups were committed to profit goals and expansion policies which had been attainable in a fast-growing economy like that of the 1950s or 1960s, but no more. While their operating costs and debt burdens soared, inflation forced interest rates on new loans to ever higher levels, and both corporations and banks were frequently swamped with liquidity problems.

Only a continued high level of consumer spending softened the economic blahs of the late 1970s. And this trend, too, was largely an inflation-born psychology which encouraged consumers to buy now and buy more, before prices could go still higher.

What it all added up to was a combination of slow, sluggish, or no real growth at all. A decade for which tremendous expansion had originally been proclaimed ended up being an economic turkey.

What can investors learn from the 1970s? The decade proves that history does repeat itself. This period was not unlike the 1910s, when the current-dollar GNP soared, but the real GNP stagnated. And, as in the 1910s, stocks moved sideways, bonds declined, and real estate prices soared. There is this important difference: since the gold price is free to float this time around, it skyrocketed.

CHAPTER THREE

The Controlling Factor

From history we have now learned that a close correlation exists between the nation's *long-term* economic trend and the way major investment markets behave. This is really not all that surprising. In the final analysis, the supply and demand in any investment market must be governed by the amount of capital being generated and by the sentiment of long-term investors. Both of these factors are greatly influenced by the underlying economic trend.

At this point, I think it's appropriate for me to differentiate long-term investors from traders and speculators. The typical long-term investor, as I see it, is literally an investor; he is not interested in playing the market. He wants his savings to grow, but only when not too much risk is involved. Once he invests in a stock, a bond, or a piece of real estate, he holds on to it for years and years. He doesn't pay much attention to daily or even monthly price fluctuations, and, if the investment is a stock, doesn't follow the company's current earnings performance too closely. He does want to know, however, how much income he can count on from that investment.

This typical investor, moreover, is a person of some means. But his exposure to current economic developments is limited to what he learns from the evening news or what he reads in the local paper—which, of course, is quite superficial. He doesn't know what the current GNP is, how many passenger cars were sold in the latest ten-day period, or where the leading economic indicators are heading; nor is he particularly anxious to find out; he has enough other things to worry about.

Don't belittle this long-term investor, however. While he is no darling of stockbrokers and real estate agents because he hardly turns over his holdings, he is part of a huge group that controls the bulk of all equity holdings as well as non-government-owned real estate. At the start of this decade, private investors and personal trusts, collectively, owned no less than $900 billion of corporate stocks, or nearly three-quarters of all shares outstanding. Hence, just how these individuals decide to deploy their capital has an overwhelming impact on the long-term trend of the major investment markets.

In contrast, the impact of traders' and speculators' transactions on the various markets is usually short-term in nature. These market players buy and sell actively, causing stocks to undergo short-term rallies and sinking spells. But in longer perspective, their actions are self-neutralizing. In other words, when they are bullish and buy stocks, they inject much money into the market in a matter of weeks or months; but when they turn bearish and sell, they often withdraw just as much capital from the market.

Financial institutions are a hybrid of investors and traders. They churn their portfolios actively, thereby causing many interim up-and-down moves for the securities involved. But they also constantly inject new funds into the various markets.

Both institutional investors and traders/speculators

differ from long-term investors in that they are highly sensitive to current economic and corporate earnings developments. In fact, it is their anticipation of, or reaction to, late-breaking changes that causes their frequent in-and-out movements. The investment sentiment of private long-term investors, on the other hand, changes very slowly. And this sentiment typically reflects the public's confidence in the nation's long-term economic prospect.

These serious investors collectively exert perhaps the strongest single force on the investment market's underlying trend. How willing and able they are to invest is directly influenced by the long-term economic condition. So we can safely assume that, if we are able to predict with some accuracy the long-term economic prospect, we can then successfully anticipate the probable behavior of the major investment markets. This may still sound like a tall order. But it really isn't.

Actually, economic forecasting is not unlike weather forecasting. Most weathermen often have trouble making accurate five-day forecasts. But they can state without hesitation that the temperature will drop between summer and winter and then rise again in the next two seasons. That's because the underlying temperature is determined by the slow but sure circling of the earth around the sun.

Though less regular than the earth's rotation, the economy also follows long-term cycles. To recognize these cycles, one must isolate those factors that cause the economy to undergo long-term expansion in one period and long-term contraction in another.

There are, of course, any number of books written on this subject. But as a lay investor, you will probably find them too heavy to read. So let me just give you a little elementary insight into basic economics.

To start with, most people would no doubt agree that an ideal growth economy should work something like this:

supply and demand expand in a balanced manner. At any given time, the amount of goods and services produced is about the same as the amount being purchased. And as output increases, employment grows. The resulting gain in personal income helps finance added purchases which, in turn, lead to further increases in production and employment. Meanwhile, both corporate and personal income climb. This helps generate increased savings, providing the funds needed for new capital expansion.

In short, in an ideal economy, positive developments keep reinforcing one another to effect a continuous rise in the standard of living.

Unfortunately, things never work out that smoothly. More often than not, as the economy expands, some businessmen turn more aggressive. They increase their output a little more than before. This aggressive planning sometimes pays off. When it happens, the "forward looking" businessmen enjoy greater profits than their more conservative competitors. They then become even more ambitious and launch major capital expansion programs as well. Meanwhile, other businessmen become envious and climb onto the expansion bandwagon.

Eventually, though, too many businessmen will have followed this aggressive route. Suddenly, their warehouses become overstocked and their manufacturing facilities excessive. They find it necessary to liquidate the excess inventories, especially if bank loans must be repaid. Typically, the liquidation process involves laying off workers and shutting down plants. This lowers personal income and corporate profits. Retail demand then shrinks, as does the need for capital spending. Result: a recession.

After the correction has proceeded for some time, inventories become so reduced that, relative to the underlying consumer demand, they are inadequate. Inventory rebuilding then begins with idled plants put back into operation. Before long, an economic recovery is under way.

The above example, of course, is a super-simplified version of a complex economy. In a constantly changing world, many other important factors—housing sales, government spending, credit availability, to cite just a few— also come into play. Nevertheless, it's a fact that most recessions, including all the post-World War II ones before 1980, stemmed primarily from excess inventories.

Note, however, that these inventory-related recessions typically lasted no more than a couple of years. And the recoveries that followed invariably pushed the economy well above the prerecession levels. Indeed, in long-term perspective, that entire quarter century after World War II constituted an extended period of economic expansion. The interim recessions are really analogous to the occasional cold spells that occur within a warming winter-to-summer period.

Since we are interested mostly in long-term economic swings, we must therefore look into developments other than inventory changes.

Note in this regard that the sample recessions above do point up one important fact; to wit, economic contraction is the free market's way of correcting excesses. With that in mind, it seems perfectly reasonable to assume that whenever a contraction is unusually protracted, the excesses preceding it must have been unusually acute.

But how can the economy ever progress to such a point as to become acutely imbalanced? And how can the business community err so badly as to create a situation requiring years to correct?

Actually, extreme imbalances are not really caused by businessmen alone. They are the result of errors committed by the entire cross section of the economy, the outgrowth of slowly changing public sentiment.

The fact is, in the course of a long economic expansion, the attitudes of consumers, businessmen, bankers, and politicians all change from cautiousness to carelessness. And this change invariably finds reflection in the increasing use of credit. At some point, credit expansion becomes excessive. But whereas excess inventories can be detected by management quite readily, excessive credit expansion is something not usually recognized as being dangerous until it's too late.

Let us go back and start again from that ideal economy I discussed earlier. There, everything grows orderly and evenly. If, however, the supply of goods becomes excessive, a recession follows to correct that situation. Even so, it usually doesn't take too long for the excess *supply* to be reduced to reasonable levels, especially if the underlying demand is in an uptrend.

The same cannot be said of an economy overheated by excessive *demand* for goods and services. And excessive demand is the direct outgrowth of excessive credit expansion.

Let me elaborate. Demand, of course, is evidenced by the *purchase* of goods and services. In the old days, such purchases were paid for by the income earned by those who had worked to *produce* goods or services. Thus, in a balanced economy, the supply and demand grew hand in hand.

But in modern days, more and more demand is being financed by credit, or, in other words, future income. When one buys a car on installment, for instance, the loan secured is to be repaid by income yet to be earned for goods or services yet to be produced. As a result, that auto purchase involves demand that is not fully offset by supply. It creates an economic imbalance.

Ironically, this kind of credit buying is usually welcomed by just about everyone. Consumers like it because it enables them to enjoy at present the fruits of future labor. Businesses like it because it helps to create sales that would otherwise come much later. Bankers like it because it adds to their lending activities. And finally, politicians like it because it helps generate the "prosperity" that they have promised voters.

Unfortunately, once the economy is "hooked" on credit spending, it must have ever-increasing credit to keep its expansion going. Any reversion to simple cash transactions results immediately in a drop in sales. Thus, as credit expands, spenders mortgage more and more future income, and suppliers enjoy sales that are more and more above the level justifiable by prevailing economic conditions. While it proceeds, the economy gives a booming appearance, causing euphoria to spread. But concurrently and less conspicuously, the economic underpinning deteriorates.

The fact is, when the consumer assumes more and more debts, he becomes increasingly illiquid, having forfeited a progressively large portion of his future paychecks to meet debt retirement needs. The businessman meanwhile is misled into expanding his facilities to meet a level of demand that cannot be sustained. And all levels of government receive larger than normal tax revenues, inducing politicians to spend more than future income can support. While it's difficult to pinpoint precisely when credit expansion reaches the danger point, there's no denying that if it goes on and on, the economy must eventually become acutely imbalanced.

Private consumers are by no means the only credit users. As a matter of fact, business and government units depend on credit even more. Let me hasten to point out that the use of borrowed money does not always result in economic imbalances. When bank loans serve to transfer purchasing power from one group to another, thereby making otherwise idle money more productive, they really have quite a beneficial effect.

Similarly, when a corporation floats a bond issue, it in effect borrows money from the bond buyers. The transaction removes buying power from the investor, transferring it to the issuing company. No net increase in total demand is thus created. Moreover, the bond-issuing company probably applies the proceeds to build new manufacturing plants, which ultimately help increase the supply of goods manufactured by that firm.

Most business firms, for that matter, frequently borrow from banks for current operational needs. Typically, the loans help finance the cost of building inventories. As such, they serve to increase the supply of goods. Moreover, those loans are usually repaid as soon as the goods involved are sold. Thus, temporary purchasing power created by the loan will have been cancelled by the repayment.

The upshot, then, is that the proper use of credit can indeed help facilitate healthy economic growth. But when credit is used only to bolster current consumption, it must sooner or later lead to serious imbalances.

This helps explain why deficit spending by the government throws the economy out of balance in the long run. Such spending adds to the demand for goods and services directly or indirectly through a variety of transfer payments. But it in no way adds to the supply. Moreover, the fiscal gap must be filled by the sales of debt securities, absorbing capital that would otherwise be used to build plants and equipment in the private sector that are needed to increase the supply of goods and services.

With all the above in mind, let us now examine how credit expansion and contraction have affected the economy in the past.

In the first decade of the century, most borrowing was done by the business sector. Commercial banks helped grease the wheels of commerce by providing loans for inventory building and other expansion purposes. Since those loans were repaid quite speedily, they helped nurture economic growth without causing inflation. Result: the first ten years of this century experienced a strong underlying economic uptrend.

To be sure, that decade witnessed a couple of money crises, which were attributable to the rather rigid structure of the banking system. In a nutshell, the money banks invest or lend to their borrowing clients comes basically from depositors. Since normally only a tiny percentage of money on deposit is ever withdrawn at any given time, banks tend to put as much money to work as possible. But for one reason or another, deposit withdrawals would at times surge suddenly, and many banks would find themselves having insufficient cash on hand to meet the withdrawal demand.

In the old days, most business loans were made on a demand basis; borrowers had to repay the banks whenever such loans were called. In periods of unusual deposit withdrawals, banks often had to "call in" such loans, thereby spreading the liquidity problem from the banking sector to commerce.

To avoid these periodic crises, the Federal Reserve System was formed in 1913. Among its many functions, the Federal Reserve Board was empowered to provide advances to member banks experiencing temporary liquidity problems. With the notable exception of the early 1930s, the system has functioned well in this capacity. Panicky runs on banks have rarely occurred.

But having a central bank as the lender of last resort has its drawbacks. It has encouraged commercial banks to follow excessively aggressive lending practices and to assume otherwise unacceptable risks. In the 1910s, as a result, inflationary consumer loans grew at an accelerated rate.

Then came World War I in the second half of the decade. Heavy military spending put the government's fiscal budget deep in the red. In 1918–19 alone, deficits totaled over $22 billion. That may not seem much by today's standards, but it was equivalent to well over 10% of the then gross national product. In terms of today's GNP, it would be equivalent to over $300 billion.

At any rate, it was the combination of the accelerated consumer debt growth and the government debt explosion that caused inflation to spiral in the 1910s. And that inflation, as we discussed in the last chapter, was the reason why the GNP grew rapidly in current dollars, but stagnated in constant dollars.

In the Roaring Twenties, the federal government behaved well, at least as far as its spending habits were concerned. Generating fiscal surpluses throughout the decade, the Treasury managed to reduce its outstanding debts by one-third—from $24 billion in 1920 to $16 billion in 1930.

At the start of the 1920s, moreover, there was also a postwar depression. It set the stage for a decade of slowing private debt growth. Results: inflation subsided and the economy expanded thereafter, healthily for much of the decade.

Toward the latter part of the 1920s, however, that orderly growth was gradually transformed into an unsustainable boom. Years of prosperity induced the public to anticipate good things to continue forever. As a result of widespread euphoria, the urge to borrow money for all sorts of purposes became unstoppable. Much has been written, of course, about the skyrocketing stock market loans which powered the speculator binge that culminated in the 1929 crash. But even more important for the economy as a whole was the accelerating surge in consumer debt. In 1928–29, total installment credit jumped from $2.32 billion to $3.52 billion—a two-year gain of some 52%.

You may recall that in the preceding chapter I noted that the economy actually turned sluggish in the late 1920s, even as the stock market fever was soaring. Similarly, that 52% surge in consumer debt took place in a two-year period when disposable income grew less than 8%. Obviously, it could not continue for very long. And it didn't.

Once the economy softened—personal income declined in 1930, in fact—the surge in consumer debt was abruptly reversed. Rapidly rising unemployment scared most consumers from making new debt-financed purchases. Meanwhile, the repayment of outstanding debts proceeded. As a result, total debt outstanding shrank.

But that's just for starters. Involuntary debt liquidation also took place, as any number of individuals found it impossible to meet their debt obligations and had to file for bankruptcy. Such filings of course, resulted in heavy losses to the creditors. At any rate, just as credit expansion brought about above-normal demand for goods and services, credit contraction caused demand to fall below normal.

It's not surprising, therefore, that the collapse in consumer demand made serious waves throughout the economy. In the early 1930s, inventories and accounts receivable both swelled out of control. Bankruptcies begot bankruptcies.

The vicious cycle reached its climax in 1933 when Franklin D. Roosevelt had to order the temporary closing of all banks. The economy recovered somewhat thereafter, but the shock of the market and economic crashes lingered on. Even as consumer debt resumed rising, many businesses took advantage of the modest recovery to further reduce their debt obligations. Thus, between 1929 and 1939 non-federal debt outstanding actually shrank by $34 billion to $141 billion.

The 1930s, of course, was the period when President Roosevelt tried to revitalize the economy by practicing Keynesian economics. The administration chalked up unprecedentedly large peacetime fiscal deficits. As a result, over the decade, total federal debt outstanding increased 150%. Still, in absolute terms, the ten-year increase came to only $25 billion, which was far less than the drop in non-federal debt. Result: total debt outstanding still underwent a net decline. And this overall credit contraction in the 1930s was the prime reason why FDR failed to pull the economy out of its rut during his first two terms as president.

In the preceding chapter, I suggested that even without World War II, the U.S. economy would have recovered nicely in the 1940s. That view, though probably at odds with conventional wisdom, is backed by the fact that credit contraction in the private sector had just about run its course in the late 1930s.

Specifically, it was in 1938 that non-federal debt reached bottom. At that point, the total stood at $140.5 billion, down from the $176.3 billion pre-Depression peak attained in 1930. But in 1939, it nudged ahead to $141.4 billion. Then, in the next two years it jumped more than $12 billion to $153.5 billion. Thus, in the three years before Pearl Harbor, non-federal debt grew over 9%. That expansion was a decisive reversal of the contraction that had taken place in the preceding eight years.

Though the Depression brought hardship to millions, those eight years of debt liquidation were just what the doctor ordered to revitalize the economy's underlying strength. From a state of being acutely illiquid in the late 1920s, most businesses and individuals had become quite

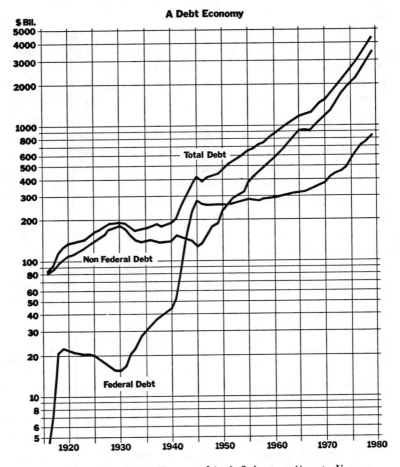

A Debt Economy

$ Bil.

Total Debt

Non Federal Debt

Federal Debt

In the 1930s, President Roosevelt's deficit spending policy resulted in a surge in total federal debt outstanding. But that
increase was offset by a contraction in private debt. As a result,
total debt was virtually unchanged for that decade. That's the
key reason why there was hardly any net growth in those ten
years.

free of debts by the late 1930s. Thus, had it not been for credit controls imposed during the war, the debt expansion in the private sector that began in 1939 would probably have continued through the 1940s. And that would surely have led to an expanding economy.

But on December 7, 1941, World War II started for the U.S. Because of a wide variety of controls, non-federal debts resumed contracting. By 1945, they were down to only $127.8 billion.

This time around, though, the contraction in private debt was altogether overshadowed by the increase in federal debt. War expenditures caused the government to sustain four years of unprecedented fiscal deficits. As a result, federal debt multiplied nearly fivefold between 1941 and 1945, skyrocketing from $57.9 billion to $278.1 billion.

Such an explosion in federal debt normally would be extremely inflationary. Indeed, consumer prices did surge in the early 1940s. But three developments helped keep the damage from becoming too devastating. The first, of course, was the imposition of price controls. But far more important was the second development: much of the government's deficits were funded by the sale of war bonds. In other words, by using their spending money to buy government securities, private Americans gave up current purchases and transferred their buying power to the government. As a result, despite the monstrous growth in federal debt, total demand really did not expand too far ahead of total supply. The third development came after the war ended in mid-1945. The federal government proceeded to achieve fiscal surpluses, thereby helping to retire some of the war debts. The upshot is that, even though the inflation rate averaged 11.5% in 1946–47, right after controls had been lifted, price stability returned by the late 1940s.

The first twenty-five years after World War II, as we've

learned earlier, was, by and large, a period of healthy economic growth. Not incidentally, it was also a period of orderly credit expansion. By and large, the memory of the crash and the Great Depression was still fresh. There was little debt-financed speculation around. Most borrowings were applied to facilitate business expansion, thereby adding to total supply as well as total demand. This explains why the entire quarter century was interrupted by only a few minor recessions and why the nation's standard of living kept rising.

The same, unfortunately, cannot be said of the ensuing decade, the 1970s. By then, the extended period of economic expansion had caused businessmen and consumers alike to throw caution to the wind. Loans secured strictly to finance current consumption or to facilitate hoarding in anticipation of rising prices thereupon proliferated. Non-federal debt expanded at an accelerating rate. In the ten years through 1979, it more than tripled—from $1,123 billion to $3,401 billion. Over the same period, by comparison, industry production rose less than 40%.

Had the credit expansion in the private sector been offset by some contraction in the public sector, things would not have been so bad. But the federal government also engaged in a buy-now-pay-later binge. Year after year, the Treasury sustained a fiscal deficit. Supposedly, most federal expenditures were mandated by Congress, so that even a responsible administration could not have achieved a balanced budget. That, of course, was untrue. If Congress had mandated certain expenditures, it could mandate their suspension, too. The fact is, Washington had gotten the bad habit of using tax money to buy votes.

At any rate, from the start of 1970 through 1979, gross federal debt climbed from $367 billion to $845 billion. The 130% increase was also many times the percentage gain in the nation's business output. Even more striking was the jump in the growth rate of federal debt itself. The average annual increase, which had equaled 1.8% in the 1950s and the 1960s, jumped to 8.8% in the 1970s.

There is no question whatsoever that the accelerated debt expansion in both the public and the private sectors brought utter malaise to the economy of the 1970s. And there is no doubt that it left some unkind legacies for the 1980s. They will be discussed in the next chapter.

The Investment Climate of the Eighties

CHAPTER FOUR

Legacies from the Seventies

From our short trip through history in Section I of this book, we have learned (1) that credit expansion and contraction typically follow a long-term cycle, (2) that this credit cycle has a lot to do with the underlying economic trend, and (3) that the long-term economic tide, in turn, determines where the best investment opportunities lie.

In other words, then, if we are able to figure out which stage of the long-term credit cycle we are in at any given time, we should be able to forecast the business climate for the ensuing years with reasonable accuracy. And knowing what economic environment to expect, we can then decide how best to prosper therein. With that in mind, let's take a closer look at the credit situation prevailing at the start of this decade and how it has affected the economy.

The decade started, of course, with credit having expanded explosively in the preceding ten years. Total debt nearly tripled from $1,491 billion to $4,246 billion. Despite that, economic growth during that decade was generally sluggish. The only thing that surged ahead was inflation. Thus, whereas consumer prices rose at an average rate of only 3.4% annually in the first two years of the decade, they soared at a rate of 11.2% in the last two. And just before it was finally curtailed by a sudden business downturn in the spring of 1980, the inflation rate had reached 17%.

Producer prices for finished goods rose equally rapidly. Their average annual increase rose from 3.5% in 1971–72 to 10.9% in 1978–79, and to over 18% in the first quarter of 1980.

Actually, credit first started to expand right after World War II, and the inflation rate started accelerating shortly thereafter. Hence, prices rose more in the 1960s than in the 1950s, and still more in the 1970s. Partly because this trend unfolded slowly, the rise in consumer prices was not considered to be too worrisome until the late 1970s. By then, however, it became by far the biggest worry confronting Americans.

Why that change? The fact that the inflation rate reached double-digit levels was, of course, noteworthy by itself. But more importantly, for the first time in decades, the inflation rate of the late 1970s exceeded the rate of personal income growth. Thus, even though the gross national product increased sharply in current dollars (and moderately in constant dollars), the real spendable income of the average worker actually started declining in 1977. This decline in purchasing power in a non-recessionary period was something altogether new in the postwar era.

But that represents only one of the economic legacies inherited by the eighties. Even more disturbing was the illiquid condition that characterized all segments of the economy. It, too, resulted from the super-rapid credit expansion of the seventies.

In the government sector, there was an absolute lack

of fiscal discipline. Throughout the seventies, the Treasury never managed to close one single fiscal year with a surplus. By the start of this decade, the Treasury debt load had become so heavy that interest payments alone accounted for well over 10% of total outlays.

Budget deficits are not merely bookkeeping statistics. Like anyone else, the government cannot really spend more money than it has. Nor can the Treasury literally "print" money. To bridge the fiscal gap, it must raise the necessary funds in the money and capital markets. This is accomplished by selling government debt securities such as Treasury bills, notes, and bonds. There is a limit, however, as to how many new offerings the market can readily absorb.

Back in the World War II years, the government also sustained huge deficits, and the Treasury had little trouble raising the necessary funds. But that's because the credit contraction of the 1930s had put consumers, businesses, and banks all in a supremely liquid position. Spurred further by patriotism, they willingly bought war bonds and other government issues offered.

Not lately, however. The rampant inflation caused by decades of credit expansion has turned investment monies into a scarce commodity. Banks have become so loaned-out that, instead of buying new Treasury issues, they have often had to liquidate their existing holdings. Thus, the Treasury has to compete in the capital market with corporations and state and local governments for money. To be sure, Washington enjoys a good competitive position; its huge taxing power renders its securities virtually risk free. But in flooding the market, the Treasury has lately made it difficult for other money seekers to satisfy their needs.

In a growing economy, corporations must have new capital to augment their working capital and to finance new expansion programs. Very often in the past, most firms were able to meet those needs by plowing their profits back into the business. And such non-cash charges as depreciation also contributed much to the internal cash flow. (Depreciation is the amount of money deducted from current revenues as an expense to compensate for the aging of fixed investments; the charge does not involve any cash outlays, but helps lower taxable income.)

During the 1970s, however, internally generated cash flow became progressively inadequate. For one thing, rapid inflation sharply increased the replacement costs of both inventories and capital plants. As a result, reported profits tended to be much overstated.

Worse yet, many companies liberalized their dividend policies. That further reduced the amount of capital available for reinvestment in the business.

Why the dividend policy change? Since the late 1960s, financial institutions have bought stocks heavily. As a result, a larger and larger portion of their portfolios is represented by corporate equities. But most stocks yielded far less than the returns available from bonds, mortgages, and other investment vehicles. And in the 1970s, there were no longer any easy capital gains to compensate for the lower current return. Unable to unload their huge holdings, the money managers pressured the companies involved into raising their dividends far more than was justified by their earnings growth.

What IBM did during that period is a good example. Back in the late 1960s, IBM's stock was regarded as such a premium growth issue that every institutional investor made sure it had a large holding in its portfolio—even though the stock provided an annual yield of less than 2%. But from early 1970 to late 1974, the stock actually declined—by nearly 50%, to the lowest level in nearly eight years. Naturally, Big Money became terribly nervous.

To placate those shareholders, IBM started liberalizing its dividend payout. Between 1974 and 1979, management boosted per-share dividend from $1.39 to $3.44 (adjusted for a 4-for-1 stock split in 1979). This 147% increase contrasts with a gain in per-share earnings over the same five-year period of less than 55%.

Sometimes, a company raises its payout simply because it has no need to retain as much of its profits for expansion purposes as it previously did. But that's not the case with IBM at all. In the late 1970s, the computer giant had to rely heavily on long-term debt financing. Thus, between 1974 and 1979, its long-term debt jumped from $336 million to nearly $1.6 billion, a nearly fivefold increase. Over the same period, shareholders' net worth rose less than 50%. (As a result of further debt financing, the company's total long-term debt approached $3 billion by late 1980.)

Relatively speaking, IBM still boasts a good balance sheet. The same cannot be said of most other companies. For manufacturers as a whole, heavy reliance on long-term debt sent the equity-to-debt ratio plummeting in the 1970s to the lowest level on record.

To be sure, corporations do not have to raise all the necessary funds from the capital market. In fact, inventories and receivables are frequently financed by bank borrowings. The trouble, however, is that in the postwar era, short-term debt has risen even more sharply than long-term debt. In more recent years, many businesses have even resorted to using bank borrowings to finance long-term undertakings. As a result, at the start of the 1980s, the short-term liabilities of non-financial corporations were almost twice as large as their holdings of liquid assets. Never since the early years of the Depression have corporations been so illiquid on this basis.

But the federal government and corporations still aren't the only groups that are heavily dependent on new

outside capital to make ends meet. State and local governments are in the same precarious boat. Actually, these
governments used to give a relatively good showing of
themselves. Many even managed to show some fiscal surpluses occasionally. That's because, until the 1970s, they
had comparatively little trouble instituting or raising
taxes. In the old days, for example, most consumers didn't
complain much when a state decided to raise its sales tax,
say from 2% to 3%. Yet, such an increase would result in
a 50% boost in tax revenues.

By the early 1970s, however, state and local governments were no longer small tax collectors. The levies they
imposed had become conspicuously burdensome. Thus,
state and local governments also had to seek outside help
to meet ever-rising expenditure needs. Though a pauper
itself, the federal government came to the rescue. Under
"revenue-sharing," it transferred tens of billions of its tax
receipts to state and local governments. But toward the end
of the 1970s, even Uncle Sam couldn't play Santa Claus
anymore. Result: municipal governments also started turning heavily to Wall Street, floating ever-increasing amounts
of tax-exempt securities.

The fact that both corporations and governments must
obtain much long-term capital is bad, but not necessarily
alarming. If private Americans save enough, they can
provide the capital needed. Their savings would be transferred to the capital seekers directly through stock and
bond investments, or indirectly via such intermediaries as
banks, insurance companies, and pension funds.

But as inflation accelerated in the 1970s, more and
more Americans were driven to hedge against further price
rises by accelerating their purchases. Many bought goods
with credit for the first time; others simply added to their
debt loads. Still others shifted their liquid assets like cash

and savings deposits into real estate, precious metals, and a wide variety of collectibles.

As a result of this rush to buy, borrow, and invest, the amount of cash being saved by Americans plunged. In the final quarter of the decade, the savings rate was only 3.3% of disposable income. In more normal times, that rate was typically twice as large. Implication: the overwhelming demand for new long-term capital by corporations and by governments of all levels can no longer be met by the amount of new saving being generated. The ever-increasing dependence on outside credit must stop.

But that's not all. A growing number of consumers are themselves beginning to have cash flow problems. Even before inflation hedge-buying became popular, most consumers had gotten hooked on the buy-now-pay-later habit. It wasn't totally their fault. The Establishment went all out to put them in that hole.

First, there was the federal government. Politicians of all stripes were anxious to make the "American dream" come true for every voter. Thus, over the years, Washington took repeated steps to make it easier and easier for Americans to own their own homes. Down payment requirements on government-guaranteed mortgages were progressively reduced, the amortization period stretched out. And to the extent it was able to do so, the Federal Reserve Board kept interest rates as low as possible, penalizing prudent savers in the process.

The government's intention was noble, of course. But soon, a large number of new homeowners found themselves saddled with huge mortgage payments they could hardly make. From the start of 1970 through the end of 1979, mortgage debt owed by households jumped from $270 billion to nearly $850 billion. The rate of increase here was double that of personal income.

The federal government wasn't solely responsible for all that, of course. The banking establishment played an even more aggressive role. Ironically, right after the Great Depression, banks had been characterized by extreme conservatism; they encouraged Americans to save for rainy days. But as early as the 1960s, a new generation of bankers, unscarred by the Depression, started to introduce go-go banking practices. To reach the people, they began opening new branches as rapidly as federal or state regulations permitted. Between 1965 and 1980, the total locations of commercial banks more than doubled.

Ostensibly, the ubiquitous banks made it easier for local people to open accounts and make deposits. But the bankers were far more interested in making consumer loans, which usually generated higher interest income than commercial loans. Hence, gushy television commercials showed the public how easy and how fast they could borrow from their friendly bankers for just about any purpose. To further prove their point, banks issued plastic credit cards liberally, not only to all who applied for them, but to many who didn't.

But let's not forget the retailers. They did their full part in inviting the public to indulge in credit buying. Auto and major appliance dealers were, of course, in the forefront. But not to be outdone were the petroleum companies, airlines, and the home furnishing industry. By the end of the 1970s, it seemed, those who bought anything other than food with cash were either foreigners or "prudes."

Besides facilitating inflation hedge-buying, credit purchases did help raise the prevailing standard of living. But they put Americans neck-deep in debt. Installment consumer credit, which totaled only $97 billion at the start of 1970, exceeded $310 billion at the end of the decade.

Unfortunately, personal income didn't rise quite so

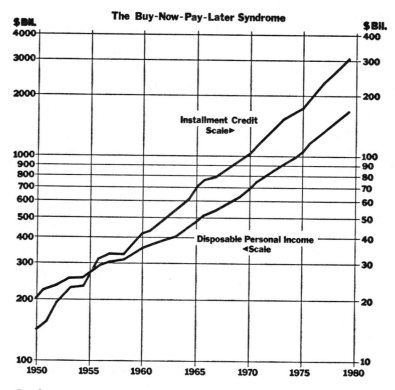

The Buy-Now-Pay-Later Syndrome

In the second half of the 1970s, Americans went on a debt-financed buying binge. Some purchases were aimed at beating inflation. Others were made simply because it was so easy and fashionable to borrow. As a result, installment credit outstanding expanded far more rapidly than disposable income. By the start of the 1980s, most middle-income consumers had become overextended.

rapidly. And because inflation continually pushed Americans into higher and higher tax brackets, disposable income grew even more slowly. As a result, the ratio of installment debt to disposable income increased at an accelerated rate. By the start of the 1980s, it reached a record 18%, up sharply from 12% ten years earlier and only 4% in 1929.

Installment debt, of course, must be paid back by the borrower sooner or later. And the record-high ratio here, together with the vigorous surge in mortgage loans discussed earlier, means that Americans, in boosting their standard of living in the 1970s, have already committed a good deal of their income yet to be earned in the 1980s.

As long as personal income keeps rising, a swelling debt load may not appear worrisome. After all, both consumer debt and mortgage loans have risen almost consistently throughout the postwar era. Though many cried wolf even in the 1960s, there hasn't been any serious dislocation.

But common sense also suggests that debt cannot increase faster than income indefinitely. At some point, the load will become excessive. And that point appears close at hand. Toward the late 1970s, the economy was still growing, though sluggishly. But both the personal bankruptcy rate and the rate of delinquent installment payments started rising steeply. Normally, this happens only after a recession has gone on for some time. The rise in these bad debt rates, I submit, represents a telltale sign that most American consumers have finally exhausted their borrowing power; some may even have become overextended. In short, like governments and corporations, private Americans have also become illiquid.

What all this means is that as the 1980s began, the long-term credit expansion cycle that started in the mid-1940s had either peaked, or was very close to peaking. Later in this book, I shall discuss what can reasonably be expected to follow. Suffice it to say here that, at best, it will extend the "stagflation" of the 1970s well into this new decade, and, at worst, it could precipitate a total financial collapse.

CHAPTER FIVE

The Economic Dichotomy

At the start of this decade there were some 575,000 millionaires in the U.S., up nearly 300% from less than 150,000 just ten years earlier. By comparison, the nation's population climbed roughly 10% during the period. If you are a member of this select group, you obviously have not been hurt by the economic malaise of the 1970s. And you have probably found it hard to relate to the family budget squeeze that I discussed in the last chapter.

As a matter of fact, a good many non-millionaires have also been relatively unscathed by the recent stagflation. They, too, have thus managed to live rather well. This is especially true for executives in big banks and large corporations. It's also true for those households in which both the husband and wife hold well-paying jobs. For this group, combined salaries of well over $50,000 annually are not at all unusual.

All this explains why luxury cars like Mercedes have continued to enjoy healthy demand, why sales of such expensive consumer goods as video recorders have been skyrocketing, and why high-priced restaurants are more often than not solidly booked.

Nevertheless, this fact does not in any way negate the conclusion that the economy is in bad shape. Even back in the 1930s, when the Great Depression was taking its heavy toll, not everyone was in financial difficulty. Park Avenue apartments in New York were then full of wealthy tenants who employed many servants. And there were enough well-to-do college students and nightclub patrons then to support the burgeoning big band industry. Hollywood stars, meanwhile, were more glamorous than ever. The point to remember, then, is that it's not unusual at all for one segment of the economy to do well, while most others don't.

Actually, a conspicuous dichotomy is itself a sign of economic imbalance. For that reason, it is usually most pronounced at the end of a major business boom. Why? In an expanding economy, the rich do literally get richer faster than the rest of the population.

For one thing, the rich get richer because they have money working for them. In the course of a credit-expansion boom, loans of all sorts increase and interest rates climb. The money borrowed by businesses and consumers is, of course, supplied by the owners through financial intermediaries. The net result is that an ever-growing proportion of the population makes ever-mounting interest payments to a relatively small group.

Note in this regard that back in the late 1940s and early 1950s, personal interest income accounted for about 4% of total personal income. By the start of this decade, that figure had grown to over 10%. Put another way, interest income grew almost three times as fast as wage and salary disbursements.

The rich get richer also because they, more than anyone else, can better afford to play the financial "long shots." Despite heavy taxation and government regulation, hard-working and innovative entrepreneurs can still get ahead in America these days. But for every new venture company that succeeds, there are many others that fall by the wayside. Thus, it is much too risky for the average investor to speculate on small untested firms. On the other hand, the rich can spread their risks by diversifying their investments; and they further reduce risks by seeking competent investment guidance. Consequently, they often benefit from ground-floor investments in the new IBMs and the new Xerox's.

But that's not all. A credit-expansion boom enriches the rich at the expense of the poor in still another way. It leads to accelerating inflation, which in turn pushes up the prices of collectibles and a wide variety of other long-term assets. Chances are, of course, that the rich own more of these items, and have originally bought them at lower prices, than most other people.

The steep surge in real estate prices during the 1970s underscores this point well. Late in that decade, the housing price surge and the accompanying rise in rental charge were among the major factors behind the then double-digit inflation. For most Americans, housing expenses absorbed more than the rule-of-thumb 25% of take-home pay. Much belt tightening became necessary.

Not so, however, for those who had bought homes years ago when prices were much cheaper and mortgage rates were much lower. Because their monthly payments were fixed at the time of original purchase, these homeowners actually incurred disproportionately small housing expenses when inflation was at its peak. As a result, they have much more money left over for discretionary spending.

Economic dichotomy is not restricted by any means to

private individuals. It's evident in the corporate sector also. While the persistent rise in corporate borrowing put most companies in an illiquid state by the start of this decade, some firms did have a surplus of cash. Oil companies, of course, were then enjoying super-lush profits; they couldn't spend them fast enough. But a large number of non-oil firms were also relatively cash rich.

To some extent, the credit for this should go to the early "wolf criers." It was back in the early 1970s when the deteriorating corporate balance sheets first became widely publicized. Then came the 1973–74 credit crunch. Many companies found themselves on the verge of insolvency. While the lesson was soon forgotten by most companies once the economy started expanding again, a few firms did take steps to upgrade their financial positions. In the late 1970s they restructured their balance sheets by selling new equities and long-term debt issues. They thus entered this decade with relatively robust working capitals.

But like millionaires, fiscally strong companies constitute a small minority. And the overall business prospect is keyed to the financial state of the great majority of individuals and corporations. In the final analysis, our economy is built on the mass market.

The same holds true for the financial market. At the start of the 1980s, as I discussed earlier, the capital market was beset by an acute shortage of newly created capital. Indeed, that shortage was the primary reason why interest rates reached double-digit levels even as business activities slowed. But as far as those money managers who handled institutional investment accounts were concerned, there was a lot of new capital around.

The dichotomy here resulted from the fact that the bulk of new money saved by private individuals across the land was funneled into a limited number of financial institutions. Instead of savings banks, they comprise mainly pension and retirement funds and insurance companies. The handful of money managers supervising their portfolios thus had tens of billions of dollars of new money every year to invest.

Nevertheless, because contributions to pension funds and insurance premium payments to insurance companies represent forced saving, the private Americans, who are the real owners of that money, can't get their hands on it. To them, making current payments on installment debt often involves selling previously bought securities. And collectively, they have more impact on Wall Street than the professional investors.

Interestingly, while the rich get richer, the poor don't *all* get poorer. Thanks to ever-rising transfer payments, those who live on government checks have also been able to increase their "income" faster than middle-income Americans. To be specific, at the start of the 1980s, transfer payments accounted for over 14% of total personal income. Three decades earlier, by comparison, their share was less than 5%. Here, too, the growth during the period was three times as fast as wages and salaries.

The upshot is that middle-class Americans, the backbone of the economy, are the ones who've been falling farther and farther behind financially in recent years.

Overseas, there is also a striking gap between the haves and the have-nots. There, a few oil-producing countries have been reaping annual surpluses that run into eleven figures. But scores of less developed countries are getting deeper and deeper into international debt. At the start of the 1980s, they owed a staggering $423 billion, so much that both the International Monetary Fund and the private banking system were reluctant to increase the loans to these LDCs much further.

Can this worldwide trend of the rich getting richer go on indefinitely at the expense of the less fortunate? No

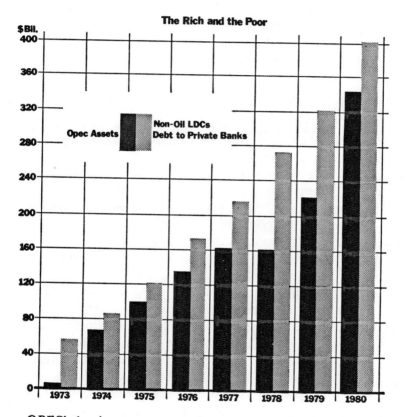

The Rich and the Poor

$Bil.

Opec Assets

Non-Oil LDCs
Debt to Private Banks

1973 1974 1975 1976 1977 1978 1979 1980

OPEC's foreign reserve assets have soared since the early 1970s. But so have the borrowings of non-oil-producing LDCs (less developed countries). At some point, many of the latter will almost surely have to default, severely hurting big Eurodollar lenders. And OPEC will indirectly be the prime victims.

way. Sooner or later, it will have gotten so far out of hand that a reversal becomes inevitable. And such trend reversals will almost always result in some dislocation.

Actually, throughout the history of civilization there were repeated periods in which a few got very rich, and a lot got very poor. Invariably, the economic imbalance would lead to widespread disorder. Finally, a redistribution of wealth would take place to pave the way for a new economic growth cycle. More often than not, though, the redistribution was the outgrowth of much bloodshed and political upheaval.

Fortunately, the capitalistic economic system is such that a redistribution of wealth can take place without any violence. The process can come (1) through an officially sanctioned debt moratorium or (2) unofficially, through widespread bankruptcy filings.

It's almost a foregone conclusion, for example, that before very long, many LDCs will default on their debts. The only question is how such defaults will affect the banking system and the creditors. Here at home, meanwhile, bankruptcy filings by both businesses and non-businesses are already on the rise. Soon, the surge will make serious waves for the creditors.

Strictly speaking, bankruptcy does not redistribute wealth. It's not like seizing the properties of rich landowners and parceling out the assets to poor farmers. But the process does cancel the liabilities of debtors and erase the assets of creditors. As a result, the poor become less poor, and the rich less rich. More important, the process enables the debtors to start reaccumulating wealth, thereby contributing to a new period of economic growth.

Considering that a distinct dichotomy does exist at present and that the widening gap must eventually be narrowed, we can safely assume that a massive wave of bankruptcies will occur some time in the 1980s. Presumably, Washington is prepared for this prospect; Congress recently passed the Bankruptcy Act of 1979, making it much easier for both private and government entities to go into receivership. Later in this book, I shall discuss its repercussions, and more importantly, how you can avoid getting hurt by such a bankruptcy wave and, indeed, profit from it.

CHAPTER SIX

The Myth of Supply-Side Economics

Unless one is quite familiar with the true economic state of the union, the recent shift toward greater fiscal conservatism in Washington is apt to create a false sense of security. One can easily conclude, for example, that since both major political parties are becoming more sympathetic to providing tax relief for business, industry will soon be able to enjoy some solid growth. No way.

The fact is, most economists, both in or out of the government, have yet to face up to the economy's most important problem—excessive credit expansion. In pushing tax relief for industry, Washington planners are merely trying something new out of desperation. Their recent efforts to shape the economy have been a disaster.

Until half a century ago, laissez-faire had been the by-word for the U.S. economy. On its own, the free-market system enabled America to show by far the most spectacular growth ever recorded. But many interim depressions did occur. Hence, when Franklin D. Roosevelt introduced his New Deal in the depth of the Great Depression, Americans readily accepted it in the belief that some guidance by Washington would help reduce the magnitude of economic swings.

Since then, both the White House and Congress have become increasingly involved in trying to manage the economy. Some planners have favored increased federal spending to bolster total demand; others, tax cuts to stimulate consumer purchases. Notwithstanding that difference, they all subscribe to the Keynesian view that the national economy can best be shaped by regulating total demand through the fiscal budget. In short, they rely mostly on controlling the rate of *credit expansion in the public sector.*

In the 1960s, another group of economic planners began to emerge. They comprised monetarists whose prime emphasis is on controlling the U.S. money supply. While they oppose economic intervention by Washington, they believe the Federal Reserve Board can and should keep the nation's money supply growing at a steady rate. New money supply is created, of course, when commercial banks extend new loans to borrowers and credit their checking accounts. In other words, therefore, the monetarists believe mainly in controlling *credit expansion in the private sector.*

In the latter part of the 1970s, the Federal Reserve tried to control the nation's money supply growth. But instead of the rigid rate that the monetarists advocated, it set growth targets in terms of a wide range, such as 4%–10% or 6%–14%. Even so, the Fed consistently failed to achieve its desired goals. The money supply expanded much too slowly in some periods, and much too rapidly in some others.

Ironically, the nation's money supply did grow quite steadily back in the early postwar decades. It was only in the late 1970s that the Fed had trouble controlling its growth. To understand why, one must remember these points: (1) new money is created when new loans are made; (2) the act of securing a loan is initiated by the borrower; and (3) the Fed's monetary policy affects the lending power of banks, not the borrowing power of consumers and businesses.

In the early postwar decades, most individuals and businesses were highly liquid, and the economy was in a major recovery phase. Thus, loan demand was always present. By controlling the reserves the banking system had, the Fed was able to control indirectly the amount of loans approved by banks. That, in turn, governed the money supply growth.

But by the late 1970s, more and more borrowers had become debt saturated. As a result, fewer and fewer bank customers were both willing *and* able to assume additional debt. Meanwhile, loan losses mounted. Thus, even when the Fed actively pumped reserves into the banking system, banks often could not find enough qualified customers applying for loans. When that happened, the money supply growth slowed. Occasionally, however, heavy loan demand would come from those major corporations which were unable to obtain long-term funds needed to finance capital investment projects. When the banks accommodated, a sudden surge in the money supply resulted.

Thus, whether or not the monetarists' theory can indeed be put into practice is still an open question. But their contention that excessive money supply growth is inflationary has become widely accepted. Meanwhile, the Keynesians were rapidly losing their following. It had become clear even to liberal politicians that deficit spending by Washington is inflationary.

The belated recognition of the root cause of inflation —demand exceeding supply—paved the way for advocates of supply-side economics to finally gain influence in Washington. The logic they present seems reasonable enough. If prices go up because demand exceeds supply, then all we have to do to stop inflation is to increase the supply.

But while it's easy to boost demand unilaterally by artificially creating new money and credit, it's quite difficult to increase supply without increasing demand at the same time. To build new plants and accumulate added inventories, industry has to buy raw materials and pay wages. The money received by the suppliers and workers involved represents new buying power, which finances new demand for goods and services. Hence, very little net increase in total supply really results.

In all fairness, the supply-side advocates also put much emphasis on enhancing productivity. In recent years, persistently decreasing productivity has made it difficult for many American industries to compete with their foreign counterparts. Automotive and consumer electronics are two glaring cases in point. According to conventional wisdom, this is the direct result of insufficient capital investments. That, in turn, has stemmed from inadequate capital formation.

To correct that situation, business leaders have launched a major lobbying campaign to convince Washington that industry must be given generous tax breaks. Increased internal cash flow, they argue, will generate added new capital for capital investment, and with more money to invest in modern facilities, American firms will regain their competitive edge.

The lobbyists have further stressed that new plants will not only result in many new hirings, but will produce a lot more goods for both the domestic and the world markets as well. In short, giving tax relief to businesses will solve the unemployment problem, reduce the inflation rate, and improve our balance of trade in one fell swoop.

Actually, the economic ills of the 1970s, while they

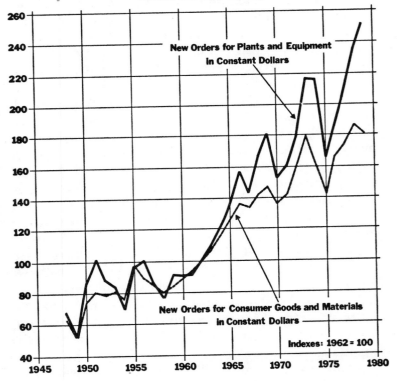

Behind The Capacity Gap

New Orders for Plants and Equipment
In Constant Dollars

New Orders for Consumer Goods and Materials
in Constant Dollars

Indexes: 1962 = 100

Orders for plants and equipment have outpaced those for con-sumer goods for over fifteen years. (Both indexes plotted above are based on constant dollars data.) This disparity contrasts sharply with the close correlation that had existed between the two prior to the mid-1960s, and explains why manufacturers have more capacity than they need.

were primarily caused by inflation, did not result from any significant shortage of production facilities. The nation's manufacturing capacity, if anything, was and is excessive. At the start of this decade, for instance, well over one-third of the nation's steel mills were idle. For manufacturers as a whole, according to the Commerce Department, unused capacity was as high as 20%. Significantly, all this prevailed at the end of a five-year economic expansion. Normally, unused capacity swells only after a business contraction has gone on for some time.

One must conclude, therefore, that excessive consumption—not underinvestment—was the real culprit for the inflationary spiral of the 1970s. For that reason, it's foolhardy to combat excessive consumption with excessive capital investment. Indeed, the free market knows better. The economic slump that started in early 1980 was the market's way of correcting the real problem.

In a balanced economy, individuals and businesses alike produce goods and services and earn income for their output. Thus, the demand financed by their income is always counterbalanced by the supply generated by their labor. As long as the two factors expand on an even keel, the economy can enjoy both healthy growth and stable prices.

But the economy is hardly ever balanced. Indeed, conditions got more and more lopsided throughout the 1970s. The accelerated rise in transfer payments was one reason. Between 1969 and 1979, social security and veterans' benefits and direct relief jumped 279%. By comparison, wages and salaries rose only 138%. Unlike earned income, these transfer payments financed demand for goods and services without augmenting supply. Presumably, this is part of America's social responsibility.

But there are imbalances in the private sector, too. Take, for instance, the auto industry. Much has been said of its failure to anticipate Americans' desire for smaller cars. But that's only half of the problem. For decades, auto workers, backed by a powerful union, have succeeded in demanding and getting wages far in excess of their output. Their contracts have been such that workers laid off receive "supplementary income" from carmakers for a long period. Result: even without producing any goods whatsoever, they get paid; so, their purchases are financed.

The auto industry itself is as much to blame. One cannot fault any union or any worker in a free market for seeking the highest wage and the most benefits he can possibly get. It's up to the management to protect the company and its shareholders by rejecting undue demands even if it means undergoing a lengthy strike. But repeatedly, auto companies substituted expediency for sound management.

Until the 1970s, Detroit could afford to be generous. General Motors had always dominated the market. As such, it had adopted a consumer-be-damned policy of administering price increases at will. Other producers followed, passing their mounting wage costs along to captive car buyers. Suddenly, they found themselves priced out of the market, unable to compete with Japanese makes.

So the industry has turned to Washington for help. But limiting imports would only deny American consumers their free choice. And encouraging the industry to make further capital investments would only result in still more idle plants.

Besides excessive wages and transfer payments, of course, total demand in the late 1970s was also buoyed by excessive credit expansion. The explosive rise of consumer and mortgage loans over the past decade has already been discussed elsewhere in this book, so it needs no further elaboration here. Suffice it to say, though, that credit created by mere accounting entries again helped stimulate new demand for goods and services without any compensating increase in the supply at all.

At any rate, demand cannot exceed supply indefinitely. The free market has a way of correcting such acute imbalances. Note that transfer payments recipients were among the first to be squeezed by inflation and that auto workers were among the first to suffer widespread unemployment. Result: unit consumption by these groups started softening around the turn of the decade.

A similar free-market reaction manifested itself for consumers as a whole. Having exhausted their borrowing power, an increasing number of middle-income Americans started the 1980s by trying to live within their current income. Debt-financed demand shrank. The gap between supply and demand narrowed in response.

As I pointed out earlier, even before the business downturn started, manufacturers' unused capacity already reached 20%. By my calculations, it may well approach 30%, if not exceed it, sometime in the early 1980s. That would be the highest since the Great Depression. Surely, there's no need to provide industry with new tax relief for capital investment purposes. Big Business really wants special treatment now not to relieve inflation or to create new jobs, but to shore up their shaky balance sheets.

Meanwhile, the real problem with the economy will persist as long as a large segment of the consuming public remains heavily laden with debts. Until installment and mortgage loans are substantially reduced, consumers won't be in any position to resume buying lavishly.

Be that as it may, the advocates of supply-side economics will probably succeed in convincing Congress to enact legislation that encourages new capital investments. Chances are, the new laws will involve either an increase in the investment tax credit or an accelerated depreciation schedule.

Some form of investment credit has already been in effect for well over a decade. Under this program, a business firm investing in new capital facilities may deduct a given percentage of the cost from its federal tax liability. It is tantamount to a discount on the capital spending cost, with taxpayers making up for the difference. Those businesses that had to expand anyway have thus enjoyed a big windfall. But even many firms with ample facilities have also found the offer too good to refuse. Their unwarranted expansion programs led to the overcapacity situation discussed earlier.

At this point, if further credit is offered under some new "reindustrialization" plan, taxpayers will merely subsidize a select few growth companies that would invest in new plants with or without tax inducement. Most other firms will probably find the investment credit not enough to offset the added overhead and capital costs incurred by building unnecessary plants.

The most talked-about plan to accelerate depreciation in recent years is called "10–5–3." Specifically, it would allow newly constructed buildings to be depreciated over a period of just ten years; fixed equipment, five years; and motor vehicles, three years. Even in this age of rapid obsolescence, of course, buildings don't really become useless in ten years, nor do fixed equipment and vehicles become valueless after five and three years respectively. But proponents of this schedule argue that this unrealistic approach is necessary to compensate for inflation.

True, ever-rising replacement costs have rendered conventional depreciation schedules inadequate for cash flow purposes. But treating a symptom of an economic excess with a deliberately distorted remedy will only create new imbalances. This proposed plan assumes that the heightened inflation rate of the late 1970s will persist in the 1980s. But as I discussed earlier, the main cause of inflation—credit expansion—was already peaking at the start of this decade. After that, credit will either stay level or contract.

Once credit expansion stops, of course, total debt outstanding will show no further net increase. At that point, manufacturing capacity will become even more excessive. Why? During the credit expansion cycle, total current demand for goods and services is financed by income (I) plus credit (C). At the peak, C is especially large. The mere elimination of credit expansion after the peak would change total current demand from I + C to just I. But since industry has geared up to meet I + C, it would immediately find itself with excessive plants on hand.

In response, output must be slashed and inventories reduced. Increased unemployment, lower wages and salaries, and sharply reduced corporate profits will follow. At some point, credit contraction occurs. Specifically, the contraction results from both voluntary debt retirement and involuntary liquidation (bankruptcy). Meaning: whereas consumption in the late 1970s was financed by current income plus debt assumption, demand starting sometime in the 1980s will be backed by current income minus debt repayments. Algebraically, I + C will change into I — C, with I (income) itself probably declining. This downward shift will surely exacerbate the current overcapacity situation.

Once the overcapacity situation becomes widely recognized, capital outlays can't help but nosedive Note that capital goods manufacturers themselves typically have huge facilities that incur heavy fixed expenses to maintain. Even a small percentage drop in sales results in a sharp rise in unit costs. To get a larger share of a shrinking pie, they are likely to engage in widespread price cutting. As a result, the 10–5–3 formula—which is based on the assumption of continuing rapid inflation—will become totally out of whack with reality. To the extent that some businessmen are encouraged to add to their capital investments, this accelerated depreciation formula will only create further unneeded capacity.

The upshot is that while encouraging Americans to save more and create more new capital makes good sense, the recent emphasis on supply-side economics won't restore equilibrium to the currently lopsided economy. It may even aggravate the situation. Eventually, inflation will indeed subside—but not because of any new economic thinking. It will be strictly the result of credit contraction—an old-fashioned free-market phenomenon.

CHAPTER SEVEN

The Real Energy Picture

Before I proceed further to discuss how the credit situation will affect the 1980s, let me digress at this point to examine two other factors which are independent of credit developments, but which will nevertheless influence the economic growth rate of this new decade. They are energy and population trends.

For the first time in this nation's history, the economy's future prospect is now closely linked to the energy picture. And that picture doesn't seem all that bright. Future generations may well consider the so-called energy crises of the 1970s more of a shock to the U.S. than was the Great Depression of the 1930s. And they will have considerable justification for thinking so.

For starters, the Great Depression lasted only about a decade. But high energy prices are here to stay in your lifetime and mine; and dependence on foreign oil will keep zapping our financial resources through a good part of the 1980s.

Moreover, as I discussed earlier in this book, the Great

Depression served at least one good purpose. The credit contraction then enabled the nation to eventually restore its liquidity. In terms of its balance sheet, the economy was a whole lot sounder in 1939 than it had been in 1929.

There's no such bright silver lining behind the current energy cloud. A good many years have already passed since OPEC first flexed its muscles and quadrupled the oil price. But there is still no such thing as a cohesive national energy policy. The threat of ever-rising fuel prices, if not long lines at the gas stations, still hangs over most Americans.

One reason why the Great Depression was, in retrospect, less ominous than the oil "crisis" is that corrective free-market forces were then able to go to work. True, both the FDR administration and Congress took major steps to stimulate the economy. But those efforts merely helped to moderate the pains induced by the economic contraction. What actually cured the economy's real ill was the long-term credit contraction in the private sector of the economy. It was a free-market function that politicians didn't care for, but permitted to proceed.

In recent years, Washington has also *tried* to lessen the hurt from the energy shortage. And presumably, President Reagan will do a lot more. Nevertheless, it has so far persistently refused to let free-market forces come into play. Some controls on oil prices have been removed, to be sure. But new price ceilings and taxes and regulations have also been introduced.

Specifically, President Carter launched his "Moral Equivalent of War" in 1977 and sent Congress no fewer than 109 recommendations for action. Though elected on an anti–Big Government campaign, he was responsible for the creation of the new Department of Energy. That department has since grown to spend some $10 billion a year and to issue tens of thousands of pages of new energy regulations and guidelines. It has not stimulated the production of a single added barrel of oil.

Lawmakers on Capitol Hill have done their thing also. They enacted well over 300 energy bills which, among other things, have empowered bureaucrats to allocate gasoline from coast to coast, determine temperature settings in commercial buildings, prepare standby plans for gas rationing, and even pass out "No Drive Day" stickers to American motorists.

One result of this inept performance by our national "leaders" has been to create mass confusion among the American people. One can still start an argument any day, anywhere, simply by saying there is, or there isn't, a real shortage of petroleum in the U.S. And even now, many otherwise intelligent people are convinced that OPEC and big oil companies are making a mockery of the free enterprise system by ripping off the public.

Let me, therefore, set things straight by debunking some of the prevalent energy myths.

Myth #1   *The OPEC cartel is still arbitrarily setting*
              prices for oil.

OPEC, comprising a large number of major oil producers, is regarded as a cartel. But in this first year of the 1980s, that international organization has not really set any minimum oil prices as it did in the mid-1970s. The group no longer has a uniform price policy, and its members don't trust each other. If anything, the more moderate members have tried to limit the maximum, not minimum, quotation that other oil export countries may charge. In short, OPEC is no longer a cartel in fact.

Myth #2　　*If OPEC can be brought to its senses, petroleum prices would drop a lot.*

Compared to what oil used to sell for, current quotations are no doubt astronomical. But in the old days, Mid-
east oil was sold by Western oil companies in a buyers'
market. They didn't have to worry about depleting the
reserves under Arab lands. And their costs for pumping
and piping the petroleum were minimal. Today, the
Arabs are selling their own assets in a sellers' market. And
in a free enterprise system, they cannot be faulted for
seeking what that traffic can bear for their products. Without profit motivation, the U.S. would not have grown from
infancy into a world economic giant in less than 200 years.
And with continued profit motivation, America would not
have fallen behind as it has in more recent decades.

What constitutes a fair price for oil? In a buyers' market, the fair market price of any product is the cost of
production plus a fair margin for profit. But in a sellers'
market, the fair price should be about as high, but no
higher than, the price of possible substitute products.
Otherwise, the excessively expensive goods price themselves out of the market.

What has happened to the steel industry is instructive
in this regard. For decades, the industry's leader routinely
administered prices even though no monopoly or cartel
was involved. And for captive customers, the administered
prices keep rising. Eventually, however, manufacturers of
automobiles and major appliances turned to using alum-
inum, plastic, and a wide variety of other substitutes. Today, the steel industry finds itself burdened with excess
capacity.

Coming back to oil, note that so far no substitute energy has yet been developed which can commercially replace OPEC oil. By this criterion, we must acknowledge

that the latter is not yet too expensive in today's market condition.

Myth #3   *Big oil companies are reaping large windfalls.*

Since the domestic oil price was decontrolled, the industry's profits have indeed soared. But prices shouldn't have been controlled to begin with. The price ceiling has been the root cause of the current energy shortage. Those who understand how the free enterprise system works had long warned that keeping prices artificially low would inevitably lead to widespread shortages.

Put another way, had it not been for domestic oil price control, oil companies would have enjoyed much higher profits years ago. So it's not that recent profits are "obscenely" high; rather, previous earnings were unduly and unfairly depressed.

Myth #4   *The surge in energy costs was the prime reason for the inflation spiral of the late 1970s.*

The manyfold increase in oil prices in a period of not too many years has, of course, sharply inflated the costs of heating and transportation and other petroleum-related items. And since energy is used by all manufacturers, it has also inflated the manufacturing costs of all goods. Even so, its impact on the overall price picture should be zero.

If a given economy having a given amount of disposable income suddenly has to spend more for energy, it will simply have less money left to pay for other things. And the resulting softening of demand for those other things will cause their price to fall. And in a balanced economy, the latter's declines will fully offset the increases in energy cost.

What happened in the late 1970s, though, was that the

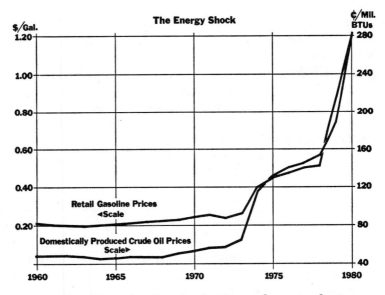

The sharp increase in oil and refined petroleum products prices has, of course, inflated the nation's energy cost. All other things being equal, consumers having to spend more on energy would have less to spend on other items. Prices of non-energy goods and services would then drop. But until recently, debt expansion has prevented free-market forces from effecting the necessary correction.

demand for "other things" didn't soften much. Encouraged by a liberal Federal Reserve Board credit policy, consumers supplemented their after-energy income with ever-rising borrowings. Here again, free-market forces were never allowed to operate.

Actually, for the world as a whole, the current oil situation is deflationary. Reason: spending money is transferred from oil-consuming countries to the oil producers. If OPEC respent all the money received, total worldwide demand for all goods and services would be stable. In reality, though, the richer OPEC members—notably Saudi Arabia—have saved some of their proceeds. Consequently, total demand has been reduced.

Myth #5   *To achieve energy independence, there must be effective laws "encouraging" Americans to cut consumption.*

There is no doubt that eliminating waste alone would go a long way toward conserving energy. But conservation *per se* is not a long-term solution; it merely stretches out the problem. Moreover, government efforts to enforce conservation only serve to convert most Americans into lawbreakers.

Take, for instance, the law hastily passed by Congress to set maximum thermostat settings in commercial buildings during the winter and minimum during the summer. It was heeded by some businessmen at the beginning, but has since been widely ignored. Even the authorities admit that they have trouble enforcing the law. Meanwhile, it's a fact that on most highways, more cars are traveling at speeds above 55 miles per hour than below.

Actually, once petroleum prices are allowed to rise freely, voluntary conservation follows naturally. In the mid-1970s, for instance, the initial quadrupling of oil prices by OPEC did not find full reflection in gasoline prices. Domestic oil prices were kept low. Hence, while the embargo then discouraged driving somewhat, car use surged back to normal once long lines at gasoline stations disappeared. In the late 1970s, by contrast, gasoline prices finally soared well above $1 a gallon. And sure enough, gasoline consumption underwent the sharpest decline on record.

Still, the decline in consumption cannot persist indefinitely. At some point, continuing conservation will stifle economic growth. A lowering of the standard of living would then result.

Myth #6   *The government should use tax credits more extensively to encourage Americans to install energy-saving devices.*

In my opinion, giving tax credits represents a misuse of the government's taxing power. It's nothing more than subsidizing special favored groups.

In recent years, for instance, the availability of tax credits may have induced many consumers to install storm windows, attic insulation, and whatever. But this artificially stimulated demand has enabled the producers of those heat-saving items to jack up prices. As a result, the consumer is really no better off. The tax credits from Washington merely become an indirect windfall to the manufacturers.

From the above facts *vs.* myths, one can readily see there really hasn't been any energy crisis as such. Yes, the economy has been retarded in recent years by a temporary energy shortage. But it's the result of years of mismanagement by Washington. That the oil industry was transformed from a buyers' market to a sellers' market is nobody's fault. It's a perfectly normal economic evolution.

Once industry and national leaders accept these facts and discard the myths, the task of increasing our energy supply will become much easier.

There is no doubt whatsoever that, with time and effort, this country will have all the energy it needs. Even right now, yet to be discovered oil both in the United States and under the continental shelf is estimated at nearly one hundred billion barrels. Granted, most of these estimates were made by the oil industry, and, whether justified or not, its credibility has lately been suspect. But even aside from oil, there are many other energy sources we can explore, if only we are willing to pay the price. Among them are natural gas, coal, and nuclear power.

In the summer of 1980 the American Gas Association estimated that with available natural gas supplies, U.S. dependence on Persian Gulf oil could be reduced 92% by 1984. To be specific, the AGA reported that about 19 trillion cubic feet of natural gas was attainable from conventional or unconventional gas wells in "secure" and "renewable" areas. This would provide the "gas energy equivalent" of 2.3 million barrels of oil per day—roughly a 500% increase over 435,000 barrels per day in 1980.

There is a kicker or two, of course. To achieve the expanded production rate by 1984, natural gas storage capacity must be greatly expanded. And supportive government regulatory actions must be forthcoming. Chances are, these prerequisites won't be met any time soon. But they certainly are easily within the U.S. ability to provide.

And then there's coal, which has often been called "an almost perfect substitute for oil." True, we have heard that song before, ever since OPEC first emerged. But the lyrics now have a fresh and clearer meaning.

Efforts to establish a new coal supply partnership between the U.S. and Western Europe have greatly accelerated. Many power plants in Europe are now being run with American coal. Others will follow suit as supply expands. Even after transatlantic shipping costs, U.S. coal is often cheaper than their own coal, far cheaper than OPEC oil, and supplies are much less risky. Delivered anywhere in the world, U.S. coal now costs less than half the price of oil per unit of energy.

As for how much coal is enough, and can we get it to market, the outlook is both bullish and buggish. In 1979, the U.S. produced a record of 770 million tons of steam coal (for power plants) and metallurgical coal (for steel-making) and was still 100 million tons below industry capacity. Annual production jumped to 815 million, tons in 1980, and estimates of 1.2 billion tons by 1990 and 2 billion tons by the year 2000 seem fully credible.

What's more, the coal boom won't be limited to the U.S. World production of raw coal was about 3.5 billion metric tons in 1980. That figure should double by 1990, then triple over the next decade. Most of this growth will occur in the U.S., Canada, Australia, and South Africa, the nations with coal reserves large enough to meet global needs. By the year 2000, Western Europe will probably import some 500 million tons annually, with another 200 million tons going to Japan.

To fulfill the world scenario for coal, of course, will require a massive international effort. Under the direction of an MIT professor, researchers from sixteen countries completed a world coal study in 1980 and found that, over the next two decades, coal can and must provide up to two-thirds of new energy needs worldwide. Huge infusions of money and technology will be required for opening new mines, shipbuilding and harbor improvements, upgraded railway systems, and other related coal delivery mechanisms.

The bottom line: coal-producing nations will need

to pay the lion's share of over $38 trillion in aggregate capital formation, and the international financial markets will have to absorb the cost—especially if the coal export markets continue to develop.

So where are the "bugs"? First, because of long lead times required at each link of the coal chain, coordinated planning is essential. So far, a lack of initiative by coal-producing nations has slowed the timetable.

Foreign coal buyers, moreover, are worried about antiquated transport systems and Washington's delay in making a major commitment to export steam coal—the boiler fuel in top demand for generating electricity. Several countries are "considering" major investments of their own money in East Coast port construction to expedite shipping out U.S. coal. Congress, the White House, and the U.S. Army Corps of Engineers have all given rhetorical support to the renovation of ports, piers, and railroads, but without getting much accomplished.

From the coal producers' viewpoint, it's equally important to have long-term contracts to support expanding production costs. Yet this need promotes a vicious cycle of sorts, because supply continuity still can't be assured to the buyers.

Meanwhile, federal regulations have been a major constraint on coal conversion activities. It's well known abroad, for example, that the ICC can—and has—approved increases in coal shipping rates, even in the middle of an export contract. The U.S. and other nations have frequently criticized OPEC members, of course, for raising prices after contracts were signed.

Far more restrictive have been environmental protection standards issued to reduce coal-burning pollutants, especially the buildup of carbon dioxide in the earth's atmosphere. Coal industry authorities, however, have made a strong case that these standards are unreasonable and now constitute a threat to "economic and national energy security."

In addition, the potential environmental hazards created by coal are now being reduced with new commercially available technology, with alternate same-site burning of coal and then gas, and with greater emphasis on energy conservation generally. With each such development, the motivation and rate of changeovers from oil to coal has strengthened substantially.

However far and fast the coal boom moves, U.S. reliance on foreign oil will also be diminished by our nuclear power capabilities. As the 1980s began, nuclear energy for peacetime purposes had been largely discredited. Events such as that at Three Mile Island in 1979 and failure to develop widely acceptable disposal facilities signaled that a real and present danger exists.

It is simply not logical to believe, however, that any nation that could resolve to safely send a man to the moon and back within one decade—and succeeded—cannot or will not resolve to conquer its acknowledged nuclear energy problems within another decade—and succeed again.

In short, the U.S. must regain its lost momentum in nuclear energy productivity, and by the end of this decade it will probably have done just that, radical no-nuke activists notwithstanding. For one thing, the start-up costs for nuclear supremacy and effective nuclear management have already been paid. For another, probably the most powerful forces in government and industry alike are heavily committed to the future growth of nuclear energy.

What remains to be accomplished is no small matter. Better fail-safe equipment and disposal remedies are desperately needed. So, too, are the kind of performance demonstrations that will restore public acceptance and neutralize fears of nuclear hazards. On all these counts, the U.S. has been painfully negligent to date.

But it may help to remember that findings of science, and the voices of prophets, have created resolvable public panics in the past. Six centuries or more ago, in fact, much of civilization was terrorized by news that the world is round. When it was perceived to be flat, you could avoid falling off by sailing only in "safe" waters. Sensible sailors had no need to worry. As this perception changed, the widespread fears changed, too—first to great uncertainty about where the downside curve would bottom out, then to great jubilation about the New World discovery.

Given another New World of sufficient nuclear power plants, science now proclaims an Age of Limitless Energy is feasible. There is an enormous amount of catching-up to be done in this decade. Yet, this is a challenge that the U.S., or any would-be major nation, cannot decline merely because adequate safeguards are not yet available. The safeguards are attainable; that much is certain. And as their effectiveness is demonstrated, public acceptance of nuclear energy will be attained as well.

At present, nuclear power has significant economic advantages over all other alternatives in the U.S. energy basket. Unlike the fossil fuels, of course, it is infinitely renewable. Moreover, electricity from nuclear plants is said by some experts to cost 60% less than that from oil-fired plants and 25% less than that from coal-fired plants. The search for improved nuclear safeguards can be expected to reduce this cost-saving advantage to some degree, perhaps considerably. Estimates of how much vary wildly, just as estimators argue endlessly about the preferential cost factors in any comparison of alternative energy sources.

But given a green light by Washington, and given enough public acceptance to proceed, it is undoubtedly true that nuclear power offers the best cost-benefit ratio for ending the energy crisis in the shortest period of time.

Some will say that hydroelectric or solar power *could* do the same job faster, safer, and more cheaply. To such claims, I can only answer that these two sources may very well have all the potential that's needed as the major energy forces for future generations. Probably they do. Still, for the 1980s, hydroelectric and solar power can only be counted on for marginal contributions to the nation's total energy needs.

For the hydroelectric and solar advocates, I would add one other caveat. During the 1990s and beyond, the entrenched market positions gained by nuclear power, coal, and natural gas *vis-à-vis* domestic oil producers will leave many Johnnies-come-lately at a tremendous disadvantage.

Some will also say the U.S. hasn't used common sense in selecting among its energy alternatives. This is probably true, too. One is irresistibly drawn to solar energy. It's clean, safe, secure, and apparently can be produced more cheaply than even nuclear power. But its technology is only partly in place. More research and development work is needed. Conflicts exist between basic collection systems. Many of solar energy's advocates have been associated with liberal or radical environmental groups in the past. And some seem more concerned about opposing nuclear power than advancing solar power's capabilities.

Equally disturbing, at this late date, is that there's great dissension within solar power's ranks over whether centralized or decentralized systems are best. Of such controversies, one of solar energy's most eminent spokesmen, Dr. Barry Commoner, has said in obvious frustration: "It's entirely possible to be in favor of solar energy and be stupid at the same time."

My own studies of U.S. and world energy needs have been extensive and independently conducted. I favor no vested or developing energy sources, except as my personal judgments may interpret the known facts. On this basis, to sum up, let me say again of the 1980s:

• Look for domestic producers to redouble their efforts to locate and develop new oil reserves—and to be highly successful in the process.

• Coal will increasingly become the energy alternative of choice, with natural gas in close pursuit.

• Nuclear energy will resurface as the decade progresses, stronger than ever, more "acceptable" than ever, and—I hope—still at a price advantage over alternatives.

• Solar energy will resolve many of its start-up problems, and after another decade or so will (along with nuclear power) usher in the Age of Limitless Energy—and, as Detroit's major advertisers say, "at an affordable price."

The upshot is that as the 1980s progress, Americans will find energy increasingly abundant. As a matter of fact, there will be occasional periods in which the prices of even oil and gas will come down a notch or two. By the mid-1980s, I suspect, even conventional wisdom will declare the energy "crisis" dead.

Interim price decreases notwithstanding, however, the cost of energy will never drop down to those cheap levels prevailing a generation or more ago. Americans must adjust to the fact that the days of cheap foreign oil are gone for good and the high cost of producing alternate energies will in fact provide a high floor for petroleum quotations.

It's not difficult for the nation to adjust to this new fact. But it does mean that, all other things being equal, the average American household must allocate more of its take-home pay directly or indirectly for energy. As such, it will have less money to spend on other goods and services. This adjustment thus necessarily involves a lowering of the standard of living for a period of time. That period started in the late 1970s, but won't be complete until well into the 1980s. In other words, the adjustment to the changing realities in the energy picture will be a major factor influencing the economic climate of this new decade.

CHAPTER EIGHT

The Impact of Demographic Changes

In 1975, the earth's population reached the 4 billion mark for the first time. And incredible as it now seems, that figure was then expected to double by the year 2000.

All through the 1960s, scientists, economists, and demographers were busy flashing a variety of alarm signals by projecting earlier trends into the future. The so-called ticking Population Bomb became one of the most familiar symbols of the environmental protection movements that dominated the early 1970s. Political leaders, educators, and news analysts alike also predicted widespread economic catastrophies resulting from the population explosion. Some gloomers and doomers even talked of imminent worldwide famine.

Those experts, however, evidently didn't do their homework. The fact is, even back in the mid-1970s, a basic change was taking place in the long-term underlying trend. While population was still getting larger each year, its *rate* of growth was falling unexpectedly.

Since that time, population forecasts have been revised considerably. They now show that, instead of reaching 8 billion by the year 2000, the world will then have less than 5.8 billion people.

At a 1979 United Nations–sponsored conference on world population trends, numerous reasons were advanced to explain this demographic phenomenon. Adoption of family-planning programs as national policy in many developing countries was seen as a major factor. Population specialists from around the world also stressed later ages for marriage, increasing divorce rates, liberalized abortion laws, decline of religious authority, and women's liberation movements. Higher costs of bearing and rearing children were frequently cited, and also a diminishing necessity for having many babies to ensure that a few will survive.

While their explanations are still not conclusive or all-inclusive, nearly everyone at the UN conference agreed that former fears about the Population Bomb were exaggerated. The end result, as one participating economist said, was "an astounding turnabout in the world's demographic fortunes."

Perhaps the most surprising aspect of this unforeseen trend has been its universality. Even in the most populous nations of Asia, Africa, and the Americas, there has been a dramatic decline in fertility rates. Some major nations, including France and West Germany, actually expected total population decreases. They have begun encouraging parents to have more children.

The changing demographic data do make one point very clear. Population growth is much like economic growth. It is heavily influenced by free-market forces. Imbalances seldom lead straight to absolute chaos. Instead, the collective reaction of all people affected will serve as a corrective force.

Here in the U.S., population growth in recent decades has followed a course very similar to that of most other nations.

The fertility rate started trending down in the early 1960s. It reached a record low of 1.75 births per woman in 1976. Almost immediately there was widespread speculation about Zero Population Growth arriving and its impact as a continuing factor in the national economy. ZPG is the theoretical point (2.1 children per woman) where live births and deaths balance out equally, and a stable population is established.

But this didn't happen and it won't—at least, not in this century. Instead of ZPG or anything like it, the total population has continued to inch upward, the reason being that, in any society, statistical equilibrium between births and deaths takes many years to accomplish. That is so even after fertility rates have fallen far enough and then remain at relatively constant low levels.

U.S. population gains, of course, are no longer as dramatic as they were during the big Baby Boom years following World War II. Between 1949 and 1959, the national census showed, total population increased from 149.1 million to 177.8 million for an overall gain of 28.7 million—the largest for any single decade in U.S. history.

During the next decade, total population rose by only 24.8 million, reaching 202.6 million in 1969. And in the 1970s the cumulative gain was just 17.9 million, as total population climbed to 220.5 million in 1979.

Recent studies by the Census Bureau show, however, that the demographic pendulum is again on the upswing. An increase of 21 million people is estimated for the 1980s, with total population reaching 241.5 million in 1989. Needless to say, that's because the fertility rate has begun showing a slight upward movement.

But these data for total population can be very deceptive. While overall population growth will be significantly faster during this decade than in the last, for example, the growth of the labor force will actually slow. Compared

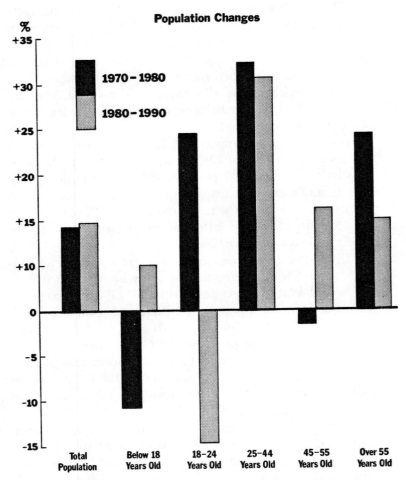

Population Changes

%

| | 1970-1980 |
| | 1980-1990 |

Total Population · Below 18 Years Old · 18-24 Years Old · 25-44 Years Old · 45-55 Years Old · Over 55 Years Old

In the 1980s, the number of people in the 18–24 age bracket will decline by over 16%—in marked contrast to the 19% growth in the preceding decade. With much fewer youngsters entering the labor market, the national work force will grow only half as rapidly as before. This will help lessen the unemployment problem, but it will also result in a reduced growth rate for national output.

with a 2.1% annual rate for 1970–80, the average annual rate of increase for 1980–90 is expected to drop to just 1.1%.

Other surprising trend changes will also occur. During the 1970s, Americans in the 18–24-year-old bracket increased by 19%—more than twice as fast as the total population. But in the 1980s, the 18–24 group will actually decline by over 16%. Since most of this age group will be entering job markets for the first time, their dwindling numbers will retard the growth of the nation's labor force.

To most economists the 25–44 age group is supposed to be the most important. That's because this segment normally spends more than any other. In the 1980s, it will grow faster than any other, with a ten-year gain expected to exceed 25%. If this age group spends the way economists expect, strongly increasing retail demand will result, thereby generating a sustained business upturn for the 1980s.

But that line of reasoning is soft on logic. A decade ago, the very same argument was also used by economists to support glowing forecasts about the 1970s. Because of an expected 28% jump in the 25–44 age group, retail demand was then supposed to soar and soar. But the "Soaring Seventies" never materialized. Over that period, unit retail sales growth actually decelerated.

What happened then was a classic example of using the wrong assumption for economic forecasting. Most forecasters assumed that the number of consumers available is directly responsible for the strength of consumer demand. The fact is, the strength of any economy, though often influenced by population trends, is not really directly determined by them. If so, overpopulated countries like China or India would surely have the strongest economies in the world.

The real key to economic growth is total income generated by real total output. The latter, in turn, is governed by the size of the labor force and its productivity. In other words, it is the product of these two changing factors that determines the real production of goods and services and the creation of new wealth and new purchasing power. Thus, the strength of an economy is keyed to its output, not to its consumption. Hence the number of consumers available is of only secondary importance.

As a general rule, the most productive workers are those in the 45–54 age group. Physically, they are not as strong as the younger adults. But, having learned to avoid mistakes from years of working experience, though not yet too old to adapt to fresh innovations, they typically generate the highest per-capita output of goods and services.

During the 1980s, growth of the 45–54 population bracket is projected at 11.5%, compared to a 2.6% drop in the 1970s. For the work force as a whole, this should mean increased average productivity. It is clearly one of the most positive demographic developments of this decade.

To recap what I've discussed so far, the composition of the U.S. labor force in the 1980s will vary greatly from that of the last decade. There'll be a tremendous decline in the 18–24 age group, a slight falling off among those aged 25–44, and a significant gain in the 45–54 age group. As a result, we'll see this most meaningful trend of all: a total labor force that is increasingly dominated by older workers.

That the labor force is growing older is not really anything new. This development has been under way for some years now. Between 1970 and 1980, the median age of the U.S. population rose from 28 to 30. In 1989 it will reach 32.5 years of age. And by the year 2000, the median age will have risen above 35.

Besides the decelerating growth in the number of younger people, the rise in the average age also reflects hefty increases in the over-65 age group. Their numbers will climb some 20% from 24.4 million in 1979 to 29.4 million in 1989. This retirement-age group will then represent more than 12% of the total population.

To be sure, many members of the 65-plus group don't want to retire, and many others can't afford to live decently without income from continued employment. And now that new laws prevent mandatory retirement before age 70, or at any age in some states, their continuing presence in the labor force is a certainty.

It's equally certain, however, that in the 1980s, the number of retirees will increase rapidly—much more so than in the 1970s.

Thus, the labor force scenario for the current decade is one of slow growth. Compared to 20% in the 1970s, it will expand by only 15% in the 1980s. That represents the slowest rate of any decade since World War II. The good news from this prospect is that the economy doesn't need to create as many new jobs as before to keep unemployment from soaring. The bad news, however, is that the growth of the nation's total output will slow.

As noted earlier, the size of the labor force is one of two key factors governing the economy's strength; the other is productivity per worker. To the extent that the number of workers in the 45–54 group is rising rapidly, this is a plus. Nevertheless, hurting productivity will be a further influx of women into the labor market. The reason for this? Most females have been entering the labor market with little or no prior working experience. On average, these new workers' initial productivity is low. During the 1970s, the proportion of families with more than one member in the labor force jumped from 52% to 64%.

This increase was the direct result of a larger number of working women around.

At first, husband-and-wife teams mushroomed because more and more women found it rewarding and challenging to hold jobs. Indeed, millions of families were able to improve their standard of living as a result. This was especially true when the husband or wife or both held relatively high-paying jobs.

But as inflation pushed living costs to budget-busting levels, an overwhelming number of housewives who would otherwise prefer to stay home simply had to work to help make family ends meet. Thus, this job-holding growth was centered in low-paying service positions. Studies show that only 6% of working women hold executive-level jobs, while 80% are employed as clerical help, salespersons, or waitresses.

As the 1980s began, some 51% of adult women already held jobs outside their homes. For the first time in American history, there were more wives working outside the home than housewives.

The percentage is likely to continue rising throughout the decade, although the growth rate may slow somewhat. (Most women able and willing to work have already entered the job market.) Thus, the labor force of the 1980s, besides growing more slowly than in the last decade, will also be characterized by a lower average output per worker. As a result, all other things being equal, economic growth will be even more sluggish than in the 1970s.

Finally, the slower labor-force growth and the sharp increase in the number of people reaching retirement age will affect the financial markets directly as well. Most pension funds will find their cash inflow rising much more slowly than in the past. A few will even see their cash flow shrinking. But for almost all funds and plans, benefit payments to retirees will increase steeply. The upshot is that in the 1980s, financial institutions will have much less new cash to invest in stocks and bonds. Some individual trusts, in fact, must liquidate existing holdings to meet their cash payment requirements. In short, a hitherto bullish market force will be gradually neutralized as this decade unfolds.

CHAPTER NINE

An Ebbing Economy

We've now established that, all other things being equal, developments relating to energy and population will by themselves cause the economy to grow more slowly in the 1980s than in the 1970s. In a nutshell, much increased direct and indirect energy costs will leave industries and consumers alike with less money to spend on other goods and services, while decelerating expansion of the work force, and the increased number of people reaching retirement age will retard the growth in total output.

But back in Chapter 4, I concluded: "As the 1980s began, the long-term credit expansion cycle that started in the mid-1940s had either peaked, or was very close to peaking." Thus, the energy and demographic developments will actually aggravate an already precarious situation, thereby hastening the inevitable reversal of the all-important credit cycle. To further understand the current credit condition, let us look at it from a different vantage point.

One way to find out just how liquid or illiquid the economy is, is to study key banking statistics. For our purpose, examining the loan-to-deposit ratio of commercial banks can be most enlightening.

It's often been said that banks lend money to borrowers just by crediting the latter's checking accounts. That's only partially true. Actually, to be able to extend loans, the banks must first have adequate lending power, and that comes from money left on deposit with them by checking or savings account customers. Thus, the loan-to-deposit ratio reveals how liquid the bank system is. A low ratio means that the system has lent out very little of the deposits on hand and thus has much unused lending power. A high ratio, on the other hand, shows that the system has become rather loaned-out.

Interestingly, this ratio also reflects the current financial condition of the non-bank sector of the economy. That's because bank loans, while they represent assets to the lenders, constitute financial obligations of the borrowers. Checking and time deposits, on the other hand, are their liquid assets. Thus, a low loan-to-deposit ratio implies that bank customers have few liabilities against their quick assets and are, therefore, highly liquid. As such, they have enormous borrowing power. The opposite holds true, of course, when the loan-to-deposit ratio is high.

It was back in the 1920s when the last credit expansion cycle reached its peak and when, as a result, inflation accelerated and economic growth slowed. That credit saturation state is well reflected in the then loan-to-deposit ratio. After having stayed within the 72%–75% range for many years, it soared to about 80% in the late summer of 1929. Even after some debt liquidation had occurred in the wake of the crash, the ratio closed that year at as high a level as 78%.

Voluntary debt repayment as well as forced loan retirement then became widespread. That credit contraction process persisted through the Depression decade and continued in the first half of the 1940s, when World War II was in progress. As to be expected, the loan-to-deposit ratio underwent a sharp plunge. Note from the accompanying chart that by 1944–45, it was as low as 19%.

That low 1944–45 ratio means that of every dollar of deposits they then had, commercial banks had loaned out less than twenty cents to borrowers. The balance was substantially invested in readily marketable U.S. Treasury securities. In short, the banking service was then super-liquid and was bursting with lending power. For depositors, that ratio also meant that more than 80% of their outstanding balances in commercial banks' checking and savings accounts were their free and clear financial assets, while less than 20% was offset by bank borrowings. Hence, bank customers were then also super-liquid and were bursting with borrowing power.

Because the combination of a decade-old depression and a colossal world war was a rare occurrence, the steep fifteen-year credit contraction was also rare. By the same token, the extreme liquidity prevailing in the mid-1940s was unusual as well.

I cannot overemphasize the importance of this point. Only by recognizing and remembering that an anomaly existed at the end of World War II can one avoid regarding the vigorous economic expansion of the ensuing decades as something normal. And only then can one refrain from expecting future business contractions to follow the typical pattern of the early postwar recessions.

Because consumer goods were in short supply during the war years, most Americans couldn't buy them even when they had the money. A growing pent-up demand resulted. Once the war ended, therefore, Americans went on a spectacular buying spree. In just five years, consumer expenditures for durable goods more than tripled. That, in turn, brought about a durable-goods-induced boom that

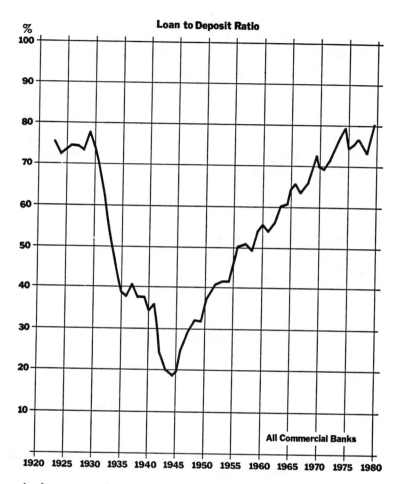

Loan to Deposit Ratio

%

All Commercial Banks

1920 1925 1930 1935 1940 1945 1950 1955 1960 1965 1970 1975 1980

At the start of this decade, total commercial bank loans were equivalent to over 80% of bank deposits. The ratio was more than four times as large as it was at the end of World War II. Meaning: in thirty-five years, the banking system has changed from being superliquid to being excessively loaned-out. The current loan-to-deposit ratio is even higher than the figure prevailing in 1929.

went a long way toward allaying the fears that had accumulated during the Depression.

From then on both consumers and businessmen became progressively less hesitant to take on debts. Their bankers also became progressively more accommodating. Helped further by lower and lower down payment requirements and easier and easier payment terms, debt-financed purchases surged, and the economy soared.

Though the postwar economy expanded rapidly, debt climbed much faster. In the thirty-five years through the end of the 1970s, the nation's gross national product multiplied eleven times, but commercial bank loans skyrocketed by nearly thirty-five times. As a result, the loan-to-deposit ratio soared. By the start of the 1980s, it stood above 80%, more than four times the level prevailing in mid-1945, and even higher than it was back in 1929!

At this point, two things are indisputable. First, the loan-to-deposit ratio cannot possibly quadruple again to 320% in the next thirty-five years, or, for that matter, even till the end of time. For all practical purposes, it has risen as high as it can go. The fact is, commercial banks must keep some money in marketable securities that can be converted into cash at a moment's notice. And they must meet reserve requirements prescribed by the Federal Reserve Board.

True, the Fed can lower these requirements, and it has done just that over the past three decades. But therein precisely lies the rub. Banks put aside so few cash assets nowadays that any moderate surge in deposit withdrawals would force many of the institutions to liquidate en masse investment holdings, many of which now have huge paper losses. (Financial institutions carry investments in Treasury issues on their balance sheets at cost, even though the market values of such holdings have, in fact, been sharply lower of late.)

Secondly, without an economic expansion fueled by galloping bank loans, the growth of bank deposits itself will also slow. The net result of the two is that, in the period ahead, total bank loans will, *at best,* rise at a much reduced rate. It also means that, *at best,* the economy will grow even more sluggishly in the 1980s than in the 1970s.

But this "best-case" scenario is not likely to materialize. Rather than continuing to expand, total credit will probably level off sometime early in this new decade. For one thing, as I noted earlier in this book, there has been a sharp increase in the number of both personal and business failures. The surge, occurring even before an economic contraction got under way in early 1980, suggests that for borrowers as a group, the debt-saturation point has been reached.

For another, most public opinion surveys revealed that, at the start of this decade, Americans were becoming increasingly pessimistic over the economic prospect. For the first time in decades, a majority of the people polled actually considered the advent of a "depression" conceivable. Inasmuch as the willingness to assume debt is closely keyed to public confidence, this new national mood implies that even of those consumers who still have unused borrowing power, more and more will soon turn cautious and foreswear debt-financed purchases.

Finally, there have been repeated credit crunches over the past dozen years or so. They took place every time the Fed tried to fight inflation by tightening credit slightly. This condition confirms that the banking system, with its limited holdings in non-loan assets, has become quite inflexible.

Thus, banks—and other lending institutions as well—will probably turn more conservative. In fact, they have to for another reason. Lately, the rise in both uncollectible loans and delinquent payments has begun to cut seriously

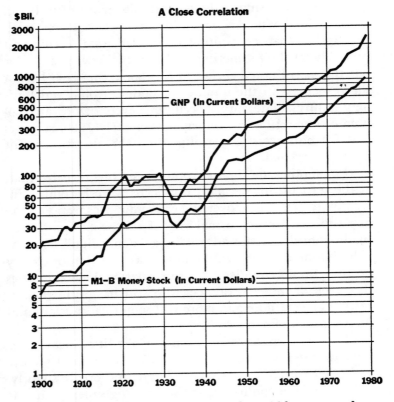

A Close Correlation

$ Bil.

GNP (In Current Dollars)

M1-B Money Stock (In Current Dollars)

Because all business transactions must be paid by money, the gross national product and the M1-B (currencies plus all checkable bank deposits) typically follow parallel moves. With the banking system unusually illiquid and credit contraction about to begin, M1-B will henceforth grow at a decelerated rate. By the same token, the nation's economic expansion must slow.

into the industry's profits. The rise here has come on top of the billions of dollars of virtually hopeless loans to underdeveloped countries, which the banks are still carrying on their books. Indeed, if these questionable assets were written off as they should be, many banks would have little or no net worth left.

To minimize further loan losses, therefore, the industry must try to improve the quality of its loan portfolio. Thus, even if the Fed keeps pumping new reserves into the system, most banks will still find it necessary to deny more and more loan applications from marginal businesses and consumers.

Any slowdown or leveling off of bank loan growth will find immediate reflection in the nation's money supply. That, in turn, will stifle any gain in economic growth, since all business transactions must be paid by money.

As a matter of fact, real money supply—that is, money supply expressed in non-inflated dollars—already started to decline in the late 1970s. Between early 1978 and mid-1980, for instance, M1-B in 1972 dollars shrank some $26 billion, or about 12%. (M1-B consists of currency plus checkable bank deposits.) That drop was one reason why delinquent payments climbed in that period. As that trend extends further into the 1980s, and it almost certainly will, the amount of money outstanding will become insufficient to facilitate all current transactions. When that happens, non-payments of outstanding bills will surely proliferate.

In this regard, I must point out that throughout the postwar period, the nation's money supply has always expanded at a slower rate than the gross national product. The difference has been made up by a faster money turnover. Inasmuch as most bills are paid with checks, this ever-increasing money velocity has been reflected in a persistent rise in the turnover of checking account deposits.

Specifically, in the first year of the 1980s, demand de-

posit turnover at New York City banks was running an un-
believable seasonally-adjusted rate of some 800 times annually. That contrasts with less than 170 times ten years
earlier and less than 25 times at the end of World War II.
New York banks, to be sure, handle mostly financial transactions. Deposits there often move from one account to
another strictly via accounting entries, and therefore turn
over much faster than money elsewhere in the economy.

Note that there are only about 250 business days in a
year. The recent turnover rate at New York banks thus implies that every dollar of deposits changed hands more than
three times a day. In other words, A would pay B, and B
would use the proceeds to pay C, and then C would pay D
all within a single business day.

To an extent, this speaks well for the efficiency of modern banking. But it also points up the vulnerability of the
whole payment process. If, for one reason or another, A is
unable to make his payment, B, C, and D won't get paid.
The stage is thus set for a massive chain reaction in the
financial world should one or more important financial
houses become insolvent.

Deposit turnover at banks outside of New York City
also accelerated sharply during the 1970s, rising from less
than 50 times to over 130 times annually. In the mid-1940s,
the rate had averaged below 14 times annually. Thus,
money in checking accounts was turning over in 1980 just
about once every two business days. While much lower
than in New York banks, this rate has also gotten about as
high as it can get.

Non–New York payments are usually made to settle
commercial transactions. And the checks involved are typically transferred from the payer to the payee through the
U.S. mail. It's a fact that for out-of-state mail, it takes two
or more days to get delivered. Until electronic banking becomes a universal practice, this slow movement of the U.S.

mail will serve to put a lid on the checking account turnover in commerce. As a matter of fact, this once-every-two-days turnover already implies that some businesses and individuals have lately been writing checks to pay overdue bills against money yet to be deposited.

Against this background, one can readily understand why the prospective slowdown in the money supply growth and the decline in real money supply can't help but lead eventually to a shortage in the medium for payments. Something has to give.

What I foresee, then, is a sharp reduction in payments for both current and past purchases. Current purchases, of course, mean current retail sales, and they will soften across the board.

The reduction in payments for past purchases will be even more disruptive, as far as the financial market is concerned. As consumers and businesses take still longer to pay their bills, almost every firm in commerce will experience a rapid rise in delinquent receivables.

Earlier in this book, I explained how industry has weakened its working capital in recent years by applying short-term funds to finance long-term projects. Now, of their already inadequate working capital, accounts receivable as well as unwanted inventories will swell rapidly. With sales and profits declining, truly quick and liquid assets will become more scarce.

Soon, the need to convert assets into cash will turn acute. Retailers will have to offer more and more rebates and clearance sales. In fact, this already started in early 1980 in such conspicuously weak sectors as automobiles and building materials. But eventually, urgent inventory liquidation will become a widespread phenomenon. At that point, the deflationary process will be in full swing.

Even so, an increasing number of businesses must still seek bank loans to help keep themselves from becoming insolvent. Short-term interest rates will then rise again. However, not every would-be borrower will be able to find friendly bankers around. So, regardless of how much reserves the Fed pumps into the banking system, bankruptcies of marginal businesses and individuals will rise.

Bankruptcies help relieve insolvent debtors from their obligations, but such born-again businesses and individuals still cannot buy enough to give the economy any meaningful boost. For the creditors, though, it means a loss of assets. In most cases, it involves the writing-off of accounts and notes receivables, which results in a further weakening of the balance sheet.

So, the liquidity squeeze is likely to snowball; the scramble for cash will get progressively urgent. Before it climaxes, the deflationary effect will be felt throughout the economy. At some point, assets to be liquidated for cash will include stocks, bonds, real estate, and collectibles, as well as business inventories.

In light of the inflationary climate that has prevailed for decades, the mere thought of deflation may seem incredible. But in a free market, prices still do respond to the supply and demand relationship. For example, in mid-1980, when inflation in general was still roaring, an oil glut caused even gasoline prices to come down a few pennies here and there.

What about labor costs? Won't union leaders keep on demanding higher wages? During the early phase of the business slowdown, they no doubt will. This is why the transition from inflation to deflation is not likely to come about speedily. But in a protracted economic contraction, militant wage demands would only result in increased unemployment. Note that in recent years, the ever-rising minimum wage has actually served to swell the number of jobless teenagers. Higher unemployment, of course, means fewer working members in unions. The latter must then shift their bargaining emphasis from wage increases to job security.

The scramble for cash and the surge in interest rates will probably climax in the early part of this decade with a massive wave of bankruptcies. This, of course, will help reverse the financial divergence discussed in the "Economic Dichotomy" chapter. After that, *voluntary* debt liquidation will probably take over as industry and individuals alike turn more conservative fiscally. While that persists, of course, the economic tide will keep ebbing.

It's difficult to predict just how long the credit contraction process will take. Much will depend on how fast debt is voluntarily and involuntarily erased. What Washington does in response will also be a factor. But because many financial safeguards have been introduced since the Great Depression, the 1980s are not likely to be anywhere as bad as the 1930s. Chances are, there won't be any across-the-board closings of banking institutions. For all practical purposes, though, a depression will be in progress.

Most people consider a depression something evil. But it really isn't 100% bad. There is a silver lining. Those who lose their jobs as a result will be badly hurt, of course. But the elimination of inflation and, indeed, the eventual emergence of deflation should prove highly beneficial to the tens of millions of Americans who are heavily dependent on more or less fixed income. More importantly, a gradual lowering of the loan-to-deposit ratio will put both consumers and corporations back on sound financial footing. The elimination of marginal manufacturers will also improve the nation's overall productivity. Once the economy becomes lean again, it will be able to resume truly solid economic growth.

CHAPTER TEN

What Can the Government Do?

In 1980, for the first time in generations, Americans elected, in Ronald Reagan, a truly pedigreed conservative to become their president. That November, conservative Republicans also made major gains in the congressional race. As a result, nearly half a century of liberal domination of the federal government was brought to an end.

Significantly, the 1980 campaign was one of those rare ones in which at least one presidential nominee actually ran on his party's platform. Reagan championed the GOP plank all the way. For that reason, the official GOP views of the economy and of Big Government presented therein should provide a reasonably reliable insight into the new administration's goals for the 1980s. The following are a few passages from that platform relating to the economy:

> *Savings and investment are the keys to economic growth. Only that part of national income which goes into savings and which is not consumed by government deficits is available to finance real economic growth.*

Americans now save less than any other people in the Western world because inflation and the high rates of taxation imposed by the Carter Administration and the Democratic Congress have destroyed their ability and incentive to save and invest. This has strangled economic growth, choked off private initiative, pushed up prices, and retarded productivity and job creation.

The sharp drop in the growth of American productivity is the main reason why Americans' average real weekly earnings are no more than they were 19 years ago.

Republicans are committed to an economic policy based on lower tax rates and a reduced rate of government spending.

Therefore, the Republican Party pledges to:

• reduce tax rates on individuals and businesses to increase incentives for all Americans and to encourage more savings, investment, output and productivity, and more jobs for Americans;

• provide special incentives for savings by lowering the tax rates on savings and investment income;

• revitalize our productive capacities by simplifying and accelerating tax depreciation schedules for facilities, structures, equipment, and vehicles;

• limit government spending to a fixed and smaller percentage of the Gross National Product; and

• balance the budget without tax increases at these lower levels of taxation and spending.

Unless taxes are reduced and federal spending is restrained, our nation's economy faces continued inflation, recession, and economic stagnation. Tax rate reductions and spending restraint will restore the savings and investment needed to create new jobs, increase living standards, and restore our competitive position in the world.

And here are a few paragraphs from the 1980 Republican platform relating to Big Government.

It is time for change—time to de-emphasize big bureaucracies—time to shift the focus of national politics from expanding government's power to that of restoring the strength of smaller communities such as the family, the neighborhood, and the workplace.

Government's power to take and tax, to regulate and require, has already reached extravagant proportions. As government's power continues to grow, the consent of the governed will diminish. Republicans support an end to the growth of the federal government and pledge to return the decision-making process to the smaller communities of society.

The emergence of policies and programs which will revitalize the free enterprise system and reverse the trend toward regulation is essential. To sustain the implementation of such policy, it is necessary to raise the public awareness and understanding that our free enterprise system is the source of all income, government and private, and raise the individual's awareness of his or her vested interest in its growth and vitality . . .

Our states and localities have the talent, wisdom, and determination to respond to the variety of demands made upon them. Block grants and revenue sharing provide local government with the means and the flexibility to solve their own problems in ways most appropriate for each locale. Unlike categorical grants, they do not lock states and localities into priorities and needs perceived by Washington. They are also more efficient because block grants and revenue sharing relieve both local government and the federal government from the costly and complicated process of program application, implementation, and review associated with the categorical grant system . . .

When we mistakenly rely on government to solve all our problems we ignore the abilities of people to solve their own problems. We pledge to renew the dispersion of power from the federal government to the states and localities. But this will not be enough. We pledge to extend the process so that power can be transferred as well to nongovernmental institutions.

There was really nothing very new in those statements, of course. What's new, however, was that in 1980 Americans finally gave the Republicans a mandate to put their philosophy into practice. The public's frustration with and disappointment in Big Government had finally reached the limit.

And this revolution at the voting booth came none too soon. In the half century through the 1970s, the government's role in the economy has grown from near zero into a monumental monstrosity. Between 1929 and 1979, to be specific, total federal purchases of goods and services skyrocketed from $1.3 billion to $167 billion—a factor of 128! Inflation contributed to the swelling figures, to be sure. But even on the same current-dollar basis, the nation's gross national product rose only twenty-three times over the same period.

But the federal government was by no means the only one that has undergone explosive growth. In the postwar period, in fact, state and local governments have grown even faster. From $8 billion in 1945, their purchases catapulted to $310 billion in 1979. As a result, at the start of this decade, combined government expenditures accounted for over 20% of the GNP.

To most Americans, the fact that Big Government has hurt the economy and fired inflation is now common knowledge. But unless you are running a business yourself, you can't begin to comprehend how millions of rules and regulations arbitrarily set by zealous bureaucrats, along with excessive taxes, have sapped the vitality of the economy.

At any rate, by the late 1970s Americans decided that enough was enough. First, Proposition 13, a referendum limiting property taxes in California, was overwhelmingly approved by voters. A tax revolt then spread clear across the land. When the decade of the Eighties began, all but a few proponents of Big Government had decided to go into hiding.

Still, Washington's efforts to retrench were more cosmetic than real. Some lawmakers did try to chop away at whatever new bills were proposed by Congress, the White House, or the ubiquitous lobbyists. The funding of a few programs sponsored by the extravagant Health, Education and Welfare Department was slashed. And the hiring of civil servants by the federal government had been slowed. But somehow, the more Washington tried, the worse things got.

Take, for instance, the budget for the fiscal year that ended September 30, 1980. Back in 1976, Jimmy Carter had promised during the presidential campaign to balance that budget. In March 1979, however, his Office of Management and Budget estimated that a deficit of $28 billion might have to be incurred after all. Thereafter, the estimated fiscal gap kept widening. And by the time the book was finally closed, the red-ink total was close to $60 billion!

As if that wasn't enough, Washington also devised many ways to inject itself into the economy without direct federal outlays. The 1980 bail-out of Chrysler is a case in point.

Here was a grossly mismanaged private company that was no longer able to compete freely in the marketplace. Here was a company that had agreed to pay laid-off workers so that they got more income staying home than many taxpayers could earn working full time. And here was a company that was arrogant enough to keep raising car prices even when a buyers' market existed.

In a competitive market, Chrysler deserved to go under. And for having supported such an incompetent management, creditors and shareholders alike should have paid the penalty.

But helped by the unsuspecting press, the company and its creditors succeeded in misleading the nation into believing that its failure would mean the imminent loss of hundreds of thousands of jobs. Succumbing to relentless lobbying efforts by several powerful special interest groups, Congress rushed through a program under which the government guaranteed some $1.5 billion in private loans to keep the ailing auto firm going a while longer. Ostensibly, Chrysler's new line of front-wheel-drive "K" cars should be given a chance to help pull the company back up.

Actually, even without federal help, Chrysler needn't have shut down altogether. The company could have gone into voluntary "Chapter 11" bankruptcy and reorganization. With the court protecting it from creditors, the company could have continued operations. The supermarket chain Food Fair, for instance, did just that in the late 1970s. While some money-losing outlets were discontinued, other stores have remained very much in business since.

Thus, contrary to what was being represented, Washington's hasty move did not really help Chrysler workers; it merely bailed out the company's creditors and investors. In the process, it also allocated badly needed credit to a mismanaged outfit, thereby denying it to more worthy credit seekers elsewhere in the economy. With its incompetent management staying on, Chrysler may still fail in the end.

All this explains why the decade of the 1980s started with the public having conspicuously less faith in the government's ability to bring Utopia to everyone than in the preceding half century. In turning to Reagan, Americans have thus expressed their desire for new leadership and a new government economic game plan.

Before speculating on what changes may be forthcoming, it may be helpful to review, if only very briefly, how Washington has gotten itself so involved with the economy to start with. Back in the 1930s, of course, President Franklin D. Roosevelt tried to arrest the Depression. But that's just for starters. The real problem came shortly after World War II, when Congress passed the Full Employment Act of 1946. For more than three decades, that act required the president and Congress to use all policy tools at their disposal to promote maximum employment of the U.S. labor force.

The same act also charged government with the responsibility of using fiscal and monetary policies in ways that contributed to increased production, greater purchasing power, and general economic prosperity. And it was through this act, more than any other legislation, that

Keynesian policies to increase consumer demand through federal spending gained their prominence.

But times changed. By the early 1970s, inflation and a sluggish economy began to take hold, and the gross federal debt shot up alarmingly every year. Government intervention had gone too far, caused too many problems, and was much too costly. After the severe recession of 1974–75, the consensus in Congress was that something had to be done to bolster or modify the fiscal policymaking process.

Several more years passed and finally the Humphrey-Hawkins Full Employment and Balanced Growth Act of 1978 was approved. This act explicitly identifies the priorities, objectives, and procedures for current U.S. economic policies and fiscal budgets. Here are some of its key provisos:

- Full employment at fair rates of compensation for all individuals able, willing, and seeking to work is a continuing national policy.
- Control of inflation and "reasonable" price stability are to be given priority attention by all fiscal policymakers.
- Encouragement of private and public capital formation should be emphasized to promote full employment, growth in productivity, price stability, and investment opportunities.
- Increased world trade and an improved U.S. trade balance are to be stressed in planning economic growth, along with maintaining a sound international monetary system.

In these and other respects, the Humphrey-Hawkins Act has perpetuated the basic tenets of Keynesian economics. But, at the same time, it has directed the president, Congress, and the Federal Reserve Board to take these obviously non-Keynesian actions:

• Respond to the widespread desire for reduced governmental intervention by "steady reductions" in government spending as a share of the GNP.

• Develop a balanced federal budget, consistent with other economic goals, as an annual objective of national policy.

• Rely as far as possible on the private sector to meet all economic and fiscal objectives related to this act.

Collectively, these goals and policies offer something to just about everyone: liberals or conservatives or middle-of-the-roaders. And that is probably their greatest weakness; they are not conducive to forming a cohesive national economic program whatsoever.

What's more, under the Humphrey-Hawkins Act, the president's annual economic report to Congress must always be constructed in terms of a five-year plan. This procedure is supposed to assure continuity in economic planning, but it restrains the president's fiscal maneuverability when changes are needed. For an incoming president, it may also mean that substantial portions of the fiscal budget are generally set for as much as two years after his election.

It is mostly for this reason, as well as Washington's fear of unemployment rises, that conservative reforms being sought by Reagan will probably take a long time to materialize fully. The irony is that a law passed to help resolve all of our economic problems is now limiting our ability to deal effectively with any of them.

Fortunately, President Reagan is a determined doer. And he will no doubt have the support of the Congress, which is now distinctly conservative. As soon as he has consolidated his position in Washington, he should start bringing down the size of the federal bureaucracy.

Success in this direction will, of course, be highly salutary to the economy over the long pull. But dismantling a government superstructure that took nearly half a century to build simply cannot be accomplished speedily. Immediately, it may even add to unemployment, especially when unnecessary civil servants are dismissed. No one, therefore, should be foolhardy enough to expect the Reagan administration to arrest immediately the economic downturn inherent in the credit contraction discussed earlier in this book. The free market must first correct the imbalances caused by decades of excesses.

Isn't there anything Washington can do to hasten the day of healthy economic growth? Of course, Washington can help if politicians truly recognize the basic problem besetting the 1980s; to wit, both consumers and industry are currently much too heavily in debt. To improve their balance sheets, both groups must save more and spend less. This will keep retail demand soft and business activities slow for some time, but it's a necessary evil.

One way to increase saving is to cut income taxes and remove dividends from double taxation, and—to avoid dissaving (deficit spending) by the Treasury—simultaneously lower federal spending. This apparently is what Reagan favors. Liberal critics already charge that such a plan favors the rich and penalizes the poor. But an across-the-board tax cut is decidedly far more apt to improve the economic liquidity than, say, increasing social spending and transfer payments. Reason: middle-class Americans, who constitute the large majority of taxpayers, are also the very group that has the largest debt burden.

Of course, some Americans will no doubt use the increase in take-home pay resulting from a tax cut to buy goods and services. That should help give the economy a lift. But more importantly, in a slowing economy, most businesses and consumers will probably apply the tax sav-

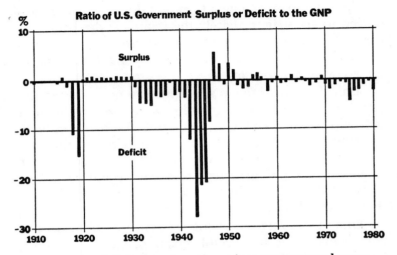

Ratio of U.S. Government Surplus or Deficit to the GNP

Surplus

Deficit

Government deficits have been large in recent years when expressed in absolute terms. But relative to the gross national product, they are nowhere as huge as they were in the 1930s and during World War II. Now, the new administration is determined to reduce the deficit. But even if it failed to do so, the federal debt expansion might not offset debt contraction in the private sector.

ings to reduce outstanding installment debt and business loans. The faster debts are reduced, the earlier the economy will regain its sound footing.

It's altogether possible that, as business slows and joblessness rises significantly, Congress will be tempted to renew its conventional efforts to prime the economic pump. Even Reagan may find it advisable to let the fiscal deficit swell. But such Washington programs will probably prove ineffective.

Earlier in this book, you may recall, I noted that back in the 1930s, despite all his liberal economic programs, FDR failed to pull the nation out of the Great Depression. The main reason, I explained, was that the contraction in private debt then was far greater than the increase in federal debt. The net debt contraction caused total demand to lag behind supply during much of that decade.

A more or less similar situation will face a good part of the 1980s. When the decade started, non-federal debt totaled $3.4 trillion. Once credit contraction takes hold, this debt could easily decline 5% or so a year for a period of time. And that would amount to a drop in non-federal debt of up to $170 billion annually. Given the new anti–Big Government mood of the public, it doesn't seem likely that the federal government will incur an annual fiscal deficit anywhere near that size any time soon. (Meanwhile, even deficits half as large would absorb so much capital as to retard the economic recovery seriously.) Indeed, even at their peak during the 1930s, annual fiscal deficits averaged a shade less than 5% of the GNP. In today's dollars, that would be equivalent to roughly $125 billion a year.

True, after World War II had started, much heavier government spending did finally give business a strong uplift. But in 1943–45, the Treasury's average annual deficit was equivalent to about 25% of the GNP. In today's terms, that would top $600 billion a year. Short of another major war, which would be too horrible even to contemplate, it's hard to imagine the Treasury ever sustaining such a fiscal gap in the 1980s.

The upshot is that there is not too much the government can do immediately to arrest the economic correction stemming from decades of credit expansion. Any artificial efforts to stimulate demand would only stretch out the correction process. For the longer pull, though, an across-the-board tax cut could help, especially if it encourages increased saving. But even here, the real beneficial impact won't be felt until the mid-1980s or later.

Revising Your Investment Thinking

CHAPTER ELEVEN

Adapting to the New Economic Climate

Inertia, or resistance to change, is a universal human characteristic. But when investments are concerned, it could also be a very costly habit. This is especially so since the 1980s require, in some cases, a complete turnaround in one's investment thinking. Unless such a change is made, in fact, building wealth in the 1980s would be quite an impossible task.

The first step toward adopting a new investment philosophy is to recognize that we are not just facing another decade of sluggish growth. Instead, we are entering an era of significant economic contraction for the first time since the 1930s. For that reason you should prepare for the advent of a depression.

Granted, the very word "depression" scares a lot of people. The mere vision of those long breadlines of the early 1930s keeps many Americans from even thinking seriously about its possibility. To make things worse, a large number of opportunists have surfaced in recent years. The tactics used by these alarmists to attract public attention have often backfired, causing the average American to regard all those who foresee a serious economic correction as irresponsible "gloomers and doomers."

Actually, not all depressions are necessarily as devastating as the one that occurred half a century ago. And because things were so bad then, chances are that the next one will be much less so. The fact is, in the aftermath of the last debacle, a large number of safeguards have been instituted.

For instance, as a result of changes made since the early 1930s, the banking system, though illiquid now, is not likely to undergo a total collapse. Hence, while many financial institutions will indeed fail in the coming depression, the average American probably won't lose his bank deposits. (I'll discuss this point in more detail later in the book.)

Similarly, though the jobless rate will reach double-digit levels, the recent trend toward more and more multiple-earner households, together with much increased government payments, will go a long way to avoid catastrophic hardship. In short, the coming depression will not destroy this country's social and economic structure as some alarmists have lately suggested.

Nevertheless, while there's no need to have undue fears, complacency is no better. An economic contraction deeper than any previous postwar recession is bound to start sometime in the early 1980s. Remember, in the wake of V-J Day, both American lenders and borrowers were unusually liquid. The vigorous economic expansion of the ensuing decades was, therefore, also unusual. Now the liquidity situation has reached the other extreme. It will take a substantial correction to put things back in balance.

Why am I talking about a coming depression, not just a bad recession? Isn't it just a matter of semantics? Not really. By my definition, a "recession" is an economic process that corrects excesses in *commerce;* a "depression" corrects excesses in *finance.*

To be more specific, a recession typically comes when businesses find themselves with excessive inventories and proceed to cut output. As long as the underlying consumer demand is growing, it usually doesn't take long before a proper balance between sales volume and stocks on hand is restored.

A depression, on the other hand, occurs when consumers find themselves having excessive debt relative to their current income and their current liquid assets. The correction takes a long time to complete if only because it necessitates a cutback in consumer purchases. The resulting decline in the underlying demand for goods and services then renders industry's inventories and plant capacities excessive, and leads to a snowballing situation.

Since I established earlier in this book that the U.S. has undergone a period of excessive credit expansion, putting most Americans deep in debt as a result, the coming economic slowdown therefore must be of the depression variety.

Once you accept the fact that a depression is inevitable, you really shouldn't have much difficulty accepting the prospect of deflation in the years ahead. I use the word "shouldn't" because I believe nevertheless that you will most likely find that hard to do, considering that prices in general have been rising for decades, and at an accelerated rate at that.

Here again, a knowledge of history may help. Prices in the United States have indeed gone up in the past two centuries more often than they have gone down. But there were at least three distinct and protracted periods when prices declined sharply and persistently. And, coincidentally or not, those periods were roughly fifty years apart.

Note in this connection that the last across-the-board price plunge took place just about half a century ago.

Frankly, I don't consider the regular recurrence of deflation in the U.S. a result of coincidence at all. Thanks to the foresight of this nation's founding fathers, the U.S. government is forbidden by the Constitution literally to print money. This fact alone sets America apart from those countries which have experienced currency collapses in the past. Instead, most of the extra money that has fostered inflation—money not resulting from the creation of wealth —has come from ballooning bank loans in the private sector. Somehow, human psychology is such that it takes about two generations for lenders and borrowers alike to make the same mistake of becoming totally overextended, and then to be penalized for the consequences in the form of depression *and* deflation.

If you are still not sure that deflation is just around the corner, may I suggest that you go back and review the logic I presented in some of the earlier chapters. Only by being truly convinced that credit expansion inevitably leads to credit contraction can you have enough conviction in the investment strategy needed to build wealth successfully in the hard times ahead. And only then can you avoid being misled by those forecasting runaway inflation for the coming years. Nothing is more dangerous to the security of your hard-earned money than to hedge against inflation just before deflation arrives.

To adapt to the new monetary climate of the early 1980s, you will also have to discard temporarily this normally correct view: interest rates fall when business slows. Chances are, at some point, just the opposite will take place. And unless you have anticipated it, the surprise could also seriously damage your investment.

Normally, interest rates decline when business slows, of course, because in a recession the demand for bank loans softens. Consumers make fewer debt-financed purchases, and businessmen have less need to accumulate inventories and carry out capital expansion plans.

Not so, however, at the final steps of a major credit expansion cycle. At that point, both long-term and short-term monies become harder and costlier to get. Money seekers then rely increasingly on non-financial sources for credit. In other words, businesses take advantage of their suppliers, and consumers, their retailers by letting their unpaid bills pile up.

You may recall that in discussing money velocity earlier in this book, I pointed out that at the start of this decade, most businesses were operating on a hand-to-mouth basis, depending urgently on current payments from receivables to make payments on overdue bills of their own. So as their receivables pile up, their cash flow slows. Given this background, any slowdown in economic activities that reduces sales and profits would further disrupt the cash flow. They must then go back to the banks for loans. Note that these borrowings are aimed at paying outstanding bills in a slow economy, not at financing expansion in a business boom. Still, they push interest rates upward just the same.

All this is by no means just a theory of mine. We are already seeing early signs of the anomaly. In the second half of 1979, bank credit was tight and the bond market was in a steep decline. As a result, non-financial business increased bank loans by just $21 billion and sold less than $12 billion of new bonds. During the period, however, it increased trade debt by over $40 billion, an all-time record by far. Early the following year, the economy started to turn downward. The plunge in the real GNP was especially steep in the second quarter. But the demand for credit to pay mounting receivables remained strong. Result: in late 1980, triple-A corporate bonds were yielding close to 13%, *up* from less than 10% in 1979; new home mortgages cost around 14%, *up* from less than 11%; three-month Treasury rates were well over 14%, *up* from the 1979 average of 10%.

There is every reason to expect this anomaly to continue until a full-scale liquidity squeeze has finally taken place. True, interest rates will drop from time to time. But as more and more receivables turn sour and outstanding loans come due, the scramble for money will become increasingly acute. Both lenders and borrowers will then realize that "cash is king." This broadening preference for cash over goods and services, as well as over long-term investments, will send the cost of money sky-high. Once again, this surge in interest rates will unfold in the face of slowing business.

In the 1980s, you must learn to be flexible. While you should anticipate a declining stock market in the earlier years, you should also prepare to capitalize on a major bull market thereafter. Similarly, you should also plan to take advantage of a dramatic reversal in the bond market. Once a full-scale liquidity squeeze has taken place, interest rates will start a long-term decline. This time around, the decline will be spurred—as it normally is—by slowing economic activities.

Unfortunately, no one can foretell at this point when the developing liquidity squeeze will climax. Much will depend on developments yet to unfold. But, when it comes, you won't miss it. The scramble for cash will result in widespread price cuts by retailers, and both personal and business bankruptcies will skyrocket. The failures of a number of big-name companies will make the evening news.

Once bankruptcy filing proliferates, most insolvent debtors will simply throw in the towel. They won't even bother to borrow anymore. From then on, loan demand for bill-paying purposes will ease. Meanwhile, as the economy keeps contracting, even well-off companies will find it prudent to reduce outstanding debts. Having no need to build new plants or stock up warehouses, they will apply whatever cash flow they have mostly to pay off borrowings.

Washington will most likely try to pump money into the economy—directly, through tax cuts, or indirectly, through the banking system. But in the wake of a much publicized liquidity squeeze, most consumers will turn fiscally more conservative. Hence, a tax cut will just increase the supply of long-term saving, and putting money into the banking system will boost the supply of short-term credit. The demand for both will remain soft. Result: a protracted trend of declining interest rates.

The decade of the 1980s will bring about a big change in most Americans' lifestyles. Having grown accustomed to nearly four decades of an ever-rising standard of living, most middle Americans will have to turn around and practice belt-tightening. Let me note once again that it won't be a matter of business executives having to sell apples on the street. But it does mean that the spending priority of the average consumer will be changed. Chances are, he will allocate more of his income to basic necessities, less to postponable goods, and much less to leisure services. To get ahead in this climate, your investment program, of course, will have to anticipate these changes.

In the remainder of this book, I will show you specifically how and when in the 1980s to build wealth by using the key investment vehicles: stocks, bonds, short-term money instruments, gold and foreign currencies, and real estate. Before that, though, let me devote a few paragraphs here to talk about collectibles.

From rare gems to T-shirts, collecting things has always been a favorite American hobby. But in recent years, many have come to regard it as a means to make money.

Most have been successful—but often only because infla-tion has accelerated. Now, things are changing.

Since the late nineteenth century, wealthy Americans have collected art treasures, antiques, diamonds, precious metals, and other rare objects on a scale the modern world had not seen before. As their acquisitive searches entered the international marketplace, in fact, all but a few great European collectors had to content themselves with left-overs.

The example of fabulous financial rewards appreciat-ing from these collections has, of course, made a lasting impact on Americans of lesser means. Gradually, as new fortunes were made and wealth itself became more gen-erally dispersed, a new breed of collectors emerged. Many are investors disenchanted with Wall Street, but interested in getting protection from inflation.

The collectibles, too, acquired a new look and greater variety. Apart from hard-money assets and the traditional museum-quality acquisitions, investors have plunged as far afield as antique coins, Chinese ceramics, Persian car-pets, classic cars, vintage wines, autographs, historical or celebrity letters, and rare books.

Collectors are buying collectibles, however, in a high-risk market. For newcomers, lack of expertise in evalua-tion or in finding alternatives is often a handicap. Strong emotional ties to particular collectibles have also helped distort supply and demand. Most of all, the market for al-most all collectibles is usually quite illiquid; the spread between the bid and ask prices is sometimes ridiculously wide.

Most collectors now fall into one of these categories:

1. Hobbyists and connoisseurs whose collections usu-ally are accumulated over a period of years. Their interest may be simply to hold and enjoy family heirlooms, to

build a collection for personal satisfaction, or to expand knowledge of a special field. Financial gain is not their primary goal. To them, therefore, the resale value is of secondary importance. The joy is in the sheer pride of possession.

2. Activist collectors who acquire tangibles they can enjoy while owning, yet who are motivated mostly by profits to be taken at some future date. They often go for highly leveraged and fast turnover deals.

3. Well-off individuals intent on preserving their capital in inflationary times. This group is basically seeking financial security; its members are most likely to make cash investments and are satisfied if the market price rises enough to offset the depreciating purchasing power of the dollar. Lately, they are most attracted to precious metal bullions and coins.

4. Institutional and corporate money managers whose goals alternate between those of the activist collectors and the preservationists. Potential financial gains are their major criteria; pride of possession is rarely a factor in their investment decisions.

Of these four groups, all but the first must accept the high risks noted earlier. Even in inflationary times, for example, liquidity can often be lost temporarily. A recession or an unexpected world event could virtually close down the secondary market for what they buy. Example: for patriotic reasons, the recent Iranian crisis has upended the once profitable market for antique Persian carpets. In times of political turmoil and economic uncertainty, moreover, the collectibles that are not portable—such as antique furnishings or classic cars or period statuary—could fall into the white-elephant category.

Fascination with collectibles will probably continue in the 1980s. But the collectors themselves will no doubt be more highly selective, increasingly conscious of security, and quicker to walk away from big price markups which dealers and individual sellers have expected in the past. Hence, at best, the markets for collectibles have peaked; profit yields will retreat. More likely than not, though, the coming liquidity squeeze and the resultant deflation will push many prices downward instead.

Hence, if you collect things strictly as a hobby, do go on collecting. But if you are interested in capital growth in the economic climate of the 1980s, I'm convinced you'll be much better off returning to the traditional investments markets, which I'll discuss in the coming chapters.

CHAPTER TWELVE

A New Era
for the Dollar
and Gold

The 1980s were ushered in by a most dramatic financial event—an explosion in the gold price. In less than three trading weeks, the London fixing soared over 60% to a record $850 per troy ounce. Quotations in New York went even higher; they reached a peak of $875. The upsurge was all the more astonishing in light of the fact that gold had already more than doubled in price in 1979, having risen from $232 to $524.

The gold fever of the 1979–80 winter attracted the attention of many Americans who had otherwise been apathetic to the metal. After that, a new breed of gold experts emerged; advertisements promoting bullion and coins started appearing in newspapers and magazines throughout the country. Even major banks and brokerage firms jumped onto the bandwagon, freely advising the public to put some money in gold. These are the same institutions that had ridiculed the "barbarous metal" when it was selling at one-tenth the price. Meanwhile, many of the perennial gold bugs have become more bullish than ever. A few have brashly suggested that the price will soon rise to $2,000 or higher.

With the metal being so widely recommended, I suddenly find myself in a lonely minority. Reason: I believe the gold price peaked in January 1980, and will now be trending downward for some time. It's much too late to join the gold rush. Instead, I think this is a good time to get rid of those old gold and silver jewelry items. (Many precious metal dealers now stand ready to buy them for the metal contents.) You can probably buy better ones back at lower prices a few years from now.

Fortunately, my role as one of the original gold advocates is still being remembered by many in the financial community. The August 4, 1980, issue of *Business Week*, for example, quoted a Wall Street executive as saying, "T. J. Holt is noted for his almost messianic faith in gold. If Holt says sell gold, you watch him."

Indeed, it was way back in 1967 when I first decided that the U.S. dollar was headed for an extended period of decline and that the gold price would soar in response. At that time, of course, gold was frozen at $35 an ounce, and both the U.S. and the International Monetary Fund insisted that the official rate would never be changed. In predicting gold's inevitable upsurge in the 1960s, therefore, I was among the first to anticipate the breakdown of the fixed-exchange rate monetary system.

For fully a dozen years thereafter, I consistently advised investors to include precious metal issues in their investment portfolios, and I repeatedly published analyses explaining why central bankers—no matter how hard they tried—could not possibly keep the price of gold from rising to its fair value. In a nutshell, I predicted that excessive credit expansion would speed up the U.S. money supply growth, which in turn would lead to accelerating inflation. I foresaw a dramatic surge in the worldwide demand for gold as a hedge against the sinking dollar and as a safe store of value—a surge that would thoroughly overwhelm the politicians. All that has since come to pass.

Lest my current "sell" advice on gold be misinterpreted, let me hasten to emphasize that I have not in any way betrayed my firm conviction that no government and no politician should ever be allowed to print money willy-nilly; nor have I modified my belief that there exists an acute need for a monetary reform to keep commercial banks from creating credit without restraint, and that, to avert a serious slump in world trade, we must soon have a new international monetary system under which deficit countries are required to settle with surplus countries through the transfer of hard and fairly valued assets.

But my conviction that a sound monetary system is vital to both the domestic and world economies should not be automatically translated into the belief that gold can be a safe and stable store of value at *any* price. And unfortunately, at well over $600, gold is now *overpriced*.

To be sure, if runaway inflation occurred and the U.S. dollar collapsed, nothing expressed in this currency can possibly be overpriced. A few generations ago, those spending millions of marks to buy any given goods in Germany fared a whole lot better than those holding on to the eventually worthless paper.

As a matter of fact, I personally witnessed the devastation caused by runaway inflation. Before I came to the States in 1947, I was studying in an American missionary college in Shanghai. Then, China's industry had been virtually demolished by World War II. Its central banks had no foreign reserves. The government literally resorted to printing money to finance its expenditures. Result: prices kept skyrocketing day after day, week after week.

In an effort to keep prices from having too many digits (a textbook, for instance, cost several thousand Chinese dollars), the government would occasionally exchange one new dollar for 100 old ones. But before we knew it, the same items would cost as much in the new currency as in the old. To help preserve their savings, even low-income laborers would exchange immediately every bit of money saved for a gold ring or whatever.

Nevertheless, there's really no way the dollar can undergo the kind of devastation that beset the French, German, and Chinese currencies earlier in this century. Strictly speaking, a currency collapses when its exchange value plunges in relation to other key currencies or monies. And such a collapse typically occurs when the central bank involved has run out of reserve assets.

The dollar, however, is by far the predominant currency in the world. It is almost universally used in international trade. In effect, therefore, the greenback is what other currencies are measured against, not vice versa. This is why on a single day, the Deutschemark could rise against the dollar while the Japanese yen declines against it.

Moreover, the dollar is a principal reserve unit. As such, it is held by almost all central banks. To suggest that the dollar will undergo a total collapse is to imply that all currencies will become worthless. Such a chaotic monetary state—which would involve a worldwide halt in all business activities except a few barter exchanges—is not even remotely probable in the years immediately ahead.

Most importantly, the U.S. still has an enormous amount of gold. Even if the metal sells at, say, $400 an ounce, the American gold stock would be worth over $110 billion. The fact is, there is more gold backing the dollar now than at any other time in nearly two decades.

Of course, even a reserve currency could collapse if the issuing government kept printing and distributing it en masse. The point to remember here, though, is that the U.S. government cannot literally print money, nor has it been issuing currency notes recklessly. Of the nation's total M5 money supply—which includes savings deposits and all other liquid assets—currency in circulation accounts for a mere 6%.

Heavy and continuing deficit spending, to be sure, is also highly inflationary. And the government has indeed been guilty of this bad habit in recent years. Still, the current "large" budget deficit is equivalent to less than 2.5% of the gross national product. It's just not large enough to bring about a dollar collapse.

The fact is, the great bulk of the nation's astronomical money supply has been created in the past few decades by the private banking system. As I explained before, when commercial banks lend money to clients, they credit the consumers' checking accounts. These bookkeeping entries create new demand deposits, which represent artificially created buying power helping to finance purchases. The inevitable result: rapidly rising prices.

It was to anticipate the repercussions from this sort of inflationary credit expansion that I recommended gold in the dozen years prior to 1980.

Now, we are at or close to the credit expansion cycle peak. Henceforth, credit growth will, at the very least, decelerate. So will the nation's money supply growth and the inflation rate. In short, the worst of the inflation spiral in this country is over. To suggest that runaway inflation is directly ahead is to play on the emotions of the unsuspecting public. And to hedge against inflation now is to fight the *last* financial war.

It shouldn't be too long, though, before the prospective slowdown in the inflation rate becomes apparent. Once that point is reached, inflation expectations will subside. The beat-inflation psychology will then become less prevalent.

Even as the U.S. inflation rate slows, price increases in

many areas abroad may still intensify. That's because the private debt structures in most foreign countries are relatively small. The buy-now-pay-later syndrome never affected the bulk of the population the way it did in the U.S. Hence, private credit contraction overseas may not be sufficient to offset debt expansion by their governments. For that reason, I fully expect *the dollar to strengthen markedly against most key foreign currencies during the 1980s*. Do not, therefore, put your money abroad as some doomers-and-gloomers suggest. The pendulum is about to swing the other way.

To be sure, because their own currencies will be depreciating, more and more foreigners will be looking for a reliable store of value as a hedge. And for centuries, gold served that purpose well. When the French and German currencies depreciated precipitously a couple of generations back, for instance, those who sought a haven in gold were the only ones who were able to keep their capital intact.

But for centuries, gold had enjoyed price stability. The Coinage Act of 1792, in effect, set the value of gold at $19.42 an ounce. Forty-two years later, an 1834 law raised it to $20.67. That figure held for a whole century until the Gold Reserve Act of 1934 raised the official price to $35 an ounce. Note that the increase over that period of nearly 150 years was modest and was consistent with the slight increase in commodity prices in general.

The $35 price prevailed from 1934 to 1971, when it was raised to $38 an ounce. Two years later, it was raised again to $42.22 an ounce. These two increases, however, failed to match the inflation that had taken place since 1934. As a result, gold was underpriced.

Actually, it was in the early 1970s that the U.S. closed its gold window, thereby severing the official link between gold and the dollar. From then on, buyers of the metal

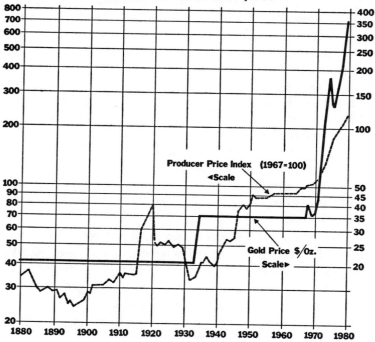

Gold: From Underpriced to Overpriced

Producer Price Index (1967=100)
◄Scale

Gold Price $/Oz.
Scale►

For centuries prior to 1970, the gold price was remarkably stable; its few advances were closely in line with that of the Producers' Price Index. Recently, however, bullion has skyrocketed far ahead of the PPI. Unless this acute overvaluation is corrected, the metal can hardly serve as a store or standard of value.

could no longer count on a fixed and steady price. Until recently, though, the open market gold price had remained undervalued; the metal, therefore, continued to constitute an ideal hedge against inflation. And that was the reason why I kept recommending investing in it through the 1970s.

The skyrocketing prices in early 1980, however, have destroyed gold's usefulness as an inflation hedge. The manyfold increase in a matter of months, which contrasted with many centuries of price stability, has made the metal not just another volatile commodity, but an overpriced one at that. *Nothing that is overpriced can ever be a safe store of value;* hence, my sell recommendation.

All this does not necessarily mean that gold will never again play an important part in the free world's monetary system. Indeed, its eventual return to a central role may be the only practical way to stop bankers and politicians alike from indulging in inflationary practices once and for all. But for gold to assume that important responsibility again, it must be reasonably priced. *Using any inflated rate as the official price would only perpetuate the inflationary sins of the 1970s.*

What, then, constitutes a fair price for gold? Let's go back to 1934 when President Roosevelt first set the official gold price at $35 a troy ounce. For nearly three decades thereafter, the U.S. economy enjoyed healthy growth, the currency market functioned efficiently, and world trade prospered. So, it's reasonable to assume that the $35 gold price was quite fair at the time it was set.

Since 1934, consumer prices have jumped roughly 450%. Over the same time span, raw materials prices have grown more—by nearly 600%. But gold, at its recent price of $665, has skyrocketed 1,800%. For all practical purposes, therefore, it has already discounted a continuation of recent inflation rates more than a decade ahead. To be consistent with the general level of prices, the gold price should really be closer to $300.

It's true that for any item, an extended period of undervaluation is more likely than not followed by a period of overvaluation. With gold having been artificially depressed at the $35 official rate until the early 1970s, its market quotation should indeed have swung well above its fair value. That's why even as recently as 1979, I still considered further price gains to be imminent.

But there's a limit to overvaluation. The blowoff usually comes when uninformed and panicky buying causes prices to gyrate violently. That, I submit, is precisely what happened in early 1980.

But what about all those strong underlying factors that most "crisis-investing" experts point to? Isn't industrial demand growing rapidly? Aren't the wealthy Arabs anxious to convert dollars into the metal? Don't central banks have a vested interest in keeping the gold price up?

Those bullish factors, which I myself used to cite as reasons to buy gold, were indeed largely responsible for pushing the gold price upward in the 1970s. But I don't expect them to continue so in the near future. Reason: the demand for gold is price-elastic.

In a competitive market, especially with a sluggish decade in prospect, industrial gold consumption is likely to grow much more slowly than in the past. Take, for instance, the highly volatile jewelry market. It reflects not only the vagaries of fashion and the changing state of the economy, but even more so, the changes in gold's price.

This has shown up dramatically in the period since 1973. Reflecting the sharp rise in gold prices in the first half of the period, world jewelry consumption fell from 999 tons in 1972 to 518 tons in 1973 and then to 225 tons in 1974. As the price of gold subsequently slid back, demand recovered strongly, rising to 523 tons in 1975 and to 935 tons in 1976. Thereafter, consumption held steady for several years. But, with a renewal of the gold price rise, jewelry usage skidded again, falling to 737 tons in 1979, and to an estimated 350 tons in 1980.

Also certain to decline as a result of the price surge is the hoarding demand from non-speculators. This includes, of course, the much publicized purchases by the Arabs. It's common knowledge that Mideastern buying was, for some time, a strong factor in the gold market. When I first called attention to that fact in mid-1976, the gold price was just slightly above $100. But the same reliable sources revealed to me that rich Arabs hardly did any buying in the 1979–80 winter, when quotations went sky-high. Unlike the Johnnies-come-lately, the Arabs are careful buyers.

Actually, one way informed and powerful investors implement a long-term acquisition program is to buy bargains when their uninformed counterparts are forced to sell in panic. Remember, the gold market is very thin. Hence, it's altogether possible at some point, when much gold is held by speculators and when such holdings are showing some paper losses, that the Arabs would suddenly unload a small portion of their large holdings just to create a snowballing selling panic. They could then turn around and pick up the pieces.

Meanwhile, most central banks would like to see gold at a *fair* price, their efforts in the 1970s to "demonetize" gold notwithstanding. If for no other reason, they still hold the bulk of all the metal ever mined. And such holdings now account for well over half of total international reserves.

But central bankers also have a vested interest in keeping any gold rush from getting too far out of hand. In early 1980, for example, the price surge was given widespread publicity. Rightly or wrongly, it was interpreted as a sign of mushrooming mistrust in paper currencies. Had that gold fever persisted much longer, a wholesale collapse in confidence might have resulted. That's something monetary leaders cannot afford.

If a new gold fever breaks out, therefore, I won't be surprised if some governmental steps will be taken to cool it. With their current massive holdings—well over $600 billion worth—major industrial countries can now indeed influence the thin gold market quite a bit.

All told, I expect the gold price to work downward in the early 1980s. The duration of the correction will depend on how steep the decline is and how many interim rallies develop. Indeed, anyone who really has faith in the free-market system can hardly conclude otherwise. Central banks can no more set an arbitrarily high official price in the future than they could depress the price in the past. The peak reached in January 1980, I therefore submit, will stand as the high for a long, long time.

Meanwhile, the prospective recovery of the dollar in the foreign-exchange market will feed on itself. As more and more dollars return from abroad, there will be a significant improvement in the U.S. balance of payments. That, in turn, will further strengthen the dollar and weaken foreign currencies and will stimulate additional dollar inflow. In the 1980s, foreign dollar holdings are likely to undergo a sharp decline.

More importantly, the return flow of the dollar will undercut many Eurodollar banks since the dollar represents the very foundation of that system. Many institutions, having made huge loans to LDCs that will never be repaid, may well go under as a result. The Arabs will probably be among the depositors to be hurt. And the world economy will contract as a result.

At some point, perhaps in the mid or late 1980s, most governments may well become totally frustrated with the protracted economic contraction. Only then will monetary leaders have a common interest in restoring order to the international monetary system, be willing to subordinate domestic political considerations to the needs for international cooperation, and be able to make solid progress toward a realistic monetary reform.

The next workable world monetary system, I believe, will restore fixed exchange rates among currencies. It will be based on a monetary unit that is both a store and a standard of value. This primary reserve unit, of course, will not be anything easily printed on paper or created by accounting entries. It will be something of lasting value.

Gold, of course, has proven its worth as something durable and portable and has been recognized worldwide for thousands of years as something of value. If, by then, the metal has regained its price stability, it could be used again as such a standard. Based on the probable money supplies outstanding in industrialized countries around 1980, I estimate that the next official price will be in the neighborhood of $300 an ounce.

CHAPTER THIRTEEN

Real Estate—
Buy, Sell, or Rent?

Ask anyone what he considers to be a surefire investment and almost invariably he will say it's buying a home. And precisely because most Americans have acted on that conviction, real estate prices have gone completely haywire, and are now exceptionally vulnerable to a liquidity squeeze. To profit in this area, you should anticipate that sometime in the 1980s—probably in the first half—real estate prices will indeed undergo a steep decline.

Before you start thinking that's absurd, remember what I said about making a complete turnaround in your investment thinking for the 1980s. True, it's understandable if you assumed that I didn't mean to include real estate in my general advice. After all, despite a series of recessions since World War II and the more recent sluggish economy, real estate values have appreciated year after year. As a result, both genuine homeowners and real estate speculators have enjoyed enormous profits. Indeed, far greater fortunes, though mostly on paper, have been made in real estate investments than on Wall Street or in any other market. (The sharp gold price rise of the late 1970s enriched only a small number of Americans.)

Behind this bubbly boom is the fact that real estate price trends are not just a function of pure and simple economics. Ownership of one's home has always been the Great American Dream. On top of this strong emotional motivation, many have also been indoctrinated since school days to believe that all real wealth comes from the land. One instinctively recoils from any suggestion that real estate will not always be a worthwhile investment.

Thus, ever since this nation emerged from the Great Depression, more and more American households have proceeded to make their real estate dreams come true. This, together with the housing shortage prevailing at the end of World War II, started pushing real estate prices persistently upward. Then, as inflation accelerated in the 1970s, private homeowners and land buyers made another discovery. As prices in general rose at double-digit rates, real estate prices climbed even faster.

Home buying for purely speculative purposes then began to proliferate. Few believed or could be persuaded to believe that the upward march in real estate prices would ever end. Regardless of how much the economy and the population grow, they rationalized, the amount of land on earth is always limited. They took for granted that there would always be enough eligible buyers around.

To make things worse, enormous sums of money poured into U.S. real estate from wealthy foreign sources in the 1970s. Prime farmland was one of their earliest targets. Later, Japanese real estate brokers became especially heavy buyers of rental properties—both private homes and apartment buildings. Oil-rich Arab sheiks then followed suit, although their presence was usually camouflaged by representation from local agents. No one knows the full extent of foreign real estate holdings. But this demand has surely been a key factor in the skyrocketing of home prices—especially in California, Florida, and Hawaii.

Adding to the demand pressure in the 1970s were corporations seeking housing for key executives or large employee groups, and institutional money managers anxious to find safe havens for their pension funds or whatever. Venture capital groups specializing in housing or land development projects also ignited real estate booms all over the country.

Real estate buying involves large sums of money, of course. But that was no problem in the 1970s. The banks kept their loan windows open to all buyers. Regardless of size, shape, or style, they accepted real estate collateral for loans they would never make at comparable margin rates in other "sound" financial transactions.

Thus, it was possible to buy land, houses, or even condominiums for zero to 10% down payments. In the commodities market, this kind of leveraging would be considered highly speculative; and in the equities market, it's legally prohibited. Where collectibles are concerned, all but the shadiest of dealers would laugh at anyone suggesting such a low-equity purchase.

But the banks willingly legitimized the low-or-nothing-down mortgage practice. It was an easy way to boost loan volume. And they were able to minimize potential losses with FHA or VA mortgage guarantees—an arrangement that protects money lenders, subsidizes builders, spreads the cost among taxpayers, and perpetuates long-term debt loads.

This high-leverage practice by no means applied only to low-cost housing. Even choice land sites or high-price homes were very seldom purchased with the 25% to 50% down payments typical of mortgages in the 1920s and 1930s. And the average repayment period for most mortgages was thirty years or more, compared with just ten years in 1929.

Many banks also formed Real Estate Investment Trusts in the early 1970s to participate in the real estate boom themselves. The REITs gained instant popularity. With Wall Street's help, they were able to attract billions of dollars from the investing public in no time. By 1973, their total assets topped $21 billion. All that extra money, of course, helped to push prices still higher.

But in 1974, a recession took place. For a while, housing and land prices remained firm, but buyers became scarce. Loan delinquencies and bankruptcies soared, and a large number of overextended REITs failed. It was the first straw in the wind in the postwar era revealing that the real estate market was far from being a no-loss proposition.

Most surviving REITs have since adjusted their portfolio mix to include more sound properties and some have resumed prospering. But toward the late 1970s, new signs of weakness began to surface elsewhere in the real estate market.

In 1979, sales of new private homes dropped over 13% to 709,000 from 817,000 the year before. Ostensibly, the drop was attributed to the then high mortgage rates. Many were hopeful that once a recession set in, easier money would revive sales activities. The economy did slow markedly in 1980, but mortgage rates climbed higher still. New home sales plummeted that spring to a seasonally adjusted annual rate of less than 450,000. Volume picked up somewhat later in the year, but it remained far, far below the lofty 1977–78 levels.

Worse yet, sales of existing homes also declined, while the supply kept piling up. According to real estate agents in most parts of the country, between 1978 and late-1980, current listings increased anywhere from 100% to 200%. Meaning: more and more houses were put on the market, but there were fewer and fewer financially qualified buyers around. Those who were especially anxious to sell for one reason or another often had to cut their asking prices by up to 20%. In these neighborhoods, deflation in home prices started.

This new trend, to be sure, was not reflected in the median sales price of either new or existing homes. Both continued to nudge ahead in 1980. But the figures were misleading. Reason: the bulk of the sales decline occurring after 1978 has been accounted for by below-$50,000 homes. Reflecting the economic dichotomy I discussed earlier, sales of $100,000+ homes held firm. The resulting change in the sales mix was what pulled the median price upward.

Given the economic and monetary scenarios for the 1980s, housing sales have little chance of staging a sustained resurgence any time soon. In the final analysis, a healthy housing demand can come only when the following requirements are met: the availability of ample mortgage money; a stable and substantial rate of new family formations; and a large number of financially qualified buyers. In the 1980s, the industry will miss on all three counts.

For openers, mortgage money will be far from ample, at least in the first part of the decade. Government and corporate demand for long-term capital will remain strong during this period, while the supply of such capital from new personal saving won't increase appreciably. Indeed, most of the prospective gain in saving will probably come through the repayment of outstanding short-term loans, which will not really enhance the supply of long-term mortgages.

The household-formation trend won't help the housing market much either. From the mid-1960s to the early 1970s, the number of new households formed each year increased at an accelerated rate. Reflecting the generally affluent society then, young Americans were willing and able to shoulder the expense of setting up their own homes. The wave of anti-Establishment feeling then also served to magnify the generation gap, further inducing young people to leave their parents. Thus, compared with an annual average of roughly 1.5% in the mid-1960s, the total number of households grew nearly 3% in the early 1970s.

Since then, however, the trend has been reversed. For one thing, the number of people in the 14–24 age group has actually declined. This, of course, has directly reduced the number of new households formed each year. Furthermore, unlike their elder brothers and sisters, these young people have rediscovered the joy of living with their parents—at the very least, it's easier on the pocketbook. A higher marriage rate among the 25–44, meanwhile, has served to combine many a pair of single households into one unit.

At any rate, by 1979, the household formation rate had dropped back to 1.7%. In absolute numbers, the 1.3 million new households formed in 1979 were down one-third from the peak 1.9 million reached just seven years earlier. Figures for 1980 won't be out for a while; but there are indications that new households probably dropped below the one million mark for the first time in more than a decade.

While the decline in household formation will keep softening the potential market for new homes, the scarcity of financially qualified home buyers will weaken it even further. The long-term economic contraction in prospect is one factor, of course, limiting the number of Americans with enough buying power. The recent surge in the cost of mortgages is another.

This fact is vividly reflected in the sharp rise in the average monthly payments required of new mortgagees. From around $200 in 1973, this average climbed above $300 for the first time in 1977, then to $380 in 1978, nearly $500 in 1979, and well over $600 in 1980. Inflation notwithstanding, personal income has hardly doubled in the same period, let alone tripled.

Note that these monthly payments do not include real estate taxes, insurance, and other assessments, which represent a hefty burden by themselves; nor do they include outlays for utilities, heating, and other maintenance. Including all these expenditures, the total outlays the average new homeowner has to make easily top $10,000 a year. Since housing expenses should account for roughly a quarter of a household's income, that total implies that the average new home buyer must now have an annual income of over $40,000. That, of course, is quite a bit higher than the average American family income, which in 1980 was close to $20,000 only.

Actually, the average American was unable to afford a new home even in the late 1970s. But prior to 1979, few buyers had any reservations about assuming ultra-heavy mortgages; they were confident that the prices of their homes would soar enough to reduce the risks involved. As a result, the ratio of mortgage debt to disposable personal income rose sharply. In 1978, it topped 60% for the first time. Back in the mid-1950s, by comparison, it had been less than 40%.

The debt load finally became much too heavy for many homeowners in 1979. The delinquency rate of residential mortgages—which had stayed close to 3% throughout the 1960s—soared to a post-Depression record of 4.6%. Remember, the economy was still expanding that year, though

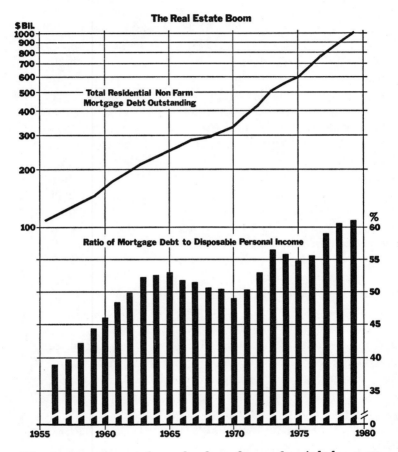

The Real Estate Boom

Total Residential Non Farm Mortgage Debt Outstanding

Ratio of Mortgage Debt to Disposable Personal Income

The recent real estate boom has been financed mainly by an explosion in mortgages. But like installment loans, mortgage debt outstanding is now equivalent to a record high percentage of disposable income. Worse yet, the delinquency rate has started to soar. Thus, a liquidity squeeze could easily bring about a collapse in real estate prices.

sluggishly. After business started slowing in 1980, the delinquency rate climbed even further, topping 5% in the first half. This finally induced mortgage lenders to screen applicants more closely, a practice they are sure to continue in the years ahead.

The upshot, then, is that the demand for new houses will gradually soften in the years ahead. And as more and more young people give up their own dwellings to rejoin their parents, the availability of existing housing units will also increase. The excessive supply over demand will mean only one thing: housing prices will come under increasing downward pressures in the years ahead. Just how much they will decline depends on (1) how urgently those who have bought for speculation will have to liquidate, and (2) how many other homeowners are forced by financial hardship to sell out.

In light of the above, here are some guidelines you may find useful in the years ahead:

• If you own a home now, are happy living in it, and foresee no difficulty making your mortgage and/or other payments even in a depression, do keep it. No amount of potential profits or savings is worth uprooting yourself and your family from your "castle." A *home* is far more than just money invested in a house.

• If you are liable to lose your job or suffer much reduced earnings in a depression, so that your ability to service your mortgage loan might be impaired, then you should sell now while the going is still reasonably good. Be realistic and try not to put too high a price tag on your home. And be prepared to accept bids that are quite a bit less than what similar homes nearby were sold for a couple of years ago.

• If you own real estate properties strictly for income purposes—that is, not for your own residence—sell them.

True, these properties may be providing you with good current rental income. But chances are you can buy these or similar properties back at much lower prices a few years hence. Meanwhile, the proceeds can bring you equally good interest income. Possible exception: you may retain these properties if their sales would result in exorbitant capital gains taxes and if you are sure that your tenants will stay in excellent financial health in the difficult years ahead.

• If you are not a homeowner at present but, for nonfinancial reasons, must buy one very soon, be sure you are able to carry your mortgage in the coming depression. Meanwhile, try to get a variable-rate mortgage. At present many bankers like this arrangement, believing that interest rates will keep trending upward. But remember, after the full-scale liquidity squeeze has taken place, interest rates will decline to levels well below recent levels. Thus, while you will have to pay high rates during the crunch, a variable mortgage will enable you to benefit at least in part from the coming deflation in the long run.

• If you must buy, buy property that is currently out of favor but is likely to enjoy renewed popularity in the late 1980s and thereafter. Keep in mind that as fewer and fewer households are formed, more and more people will tend to live under one roof. Thus, while king-sized estates are out of the question, homes with at least four bedrooms could eventually bring you a relatively higher resale value than smaller units.

• Avoid buying vacation homes in resort areas until the real estate collapse is well advanced. Recreational land is equally prone to major sell-offs. Both will be a glut on the market in the years directly ahead when luxury spending will be much reduced.

• If you want to be a homeowner but are willing to wait in order to get a better price, I suggest you rent one for now. Very often nowadays, the owners of houses for sale—especially those which have been on the market for some time—are willing to rent them out, since the income they receive can at least help offset current outlays. Thus if you find your dream home, try to arrange a rental agreement under which you have an option to buy at the current price. Such an agreement will insure you against the unlikely event that inflation persists. But note that you are not under any obligation to exercise your option to buy should home prices fall across the board and a buyers' market emerge. You can always renegotiate with the owner for a new reduced selling price, or find something else cheaper.

• If you are interested in picking up real bargains when a real estate collapse occurs, be sure you have squirreled away enough cash and other liquid assets so that you can make your move when the right time comes. It would be terribly frustrating if bargains suddenly became more available, but you found your money tied up in stocks or bonds or whatever that have also fallen in price.

• Don't buy the first "bargain" that comes around. That more and more real estate bargains will become available is inevitable. It doesn't take much price weakening before many speculators find that they owe more of their mortgage loan than the current market value of their properties. They'd then be better off turning over the ownership to the banks. And banks loaded with foreclosed homes will sooner or later have to auction them off at cut-rate prices. In extreme cases, even the banks will give up; you will then be able to buy properties by just paying off **back** taxes owed local authorities.

Bargain hunting for real estate properties may seem farfetched to you at present. But don't forget that mortgage loans have grown far more rapidly in the past decades than other kinds of debt. As a result, real estate prices are far more overpriced and real estate owners are far more illiquid than ever. Sooner or later, a liquidity squeeze will bring housing prices back down to earth.

Building Wealth in the Ebbing Eighties

CHAPTER FOURTEEN

Staying Liquid the Right Way

Until the coming liquidity squeeze has run its full course, cash is king. Holding as much cash as you can and owing as little debt as possible will not only keep you from the threat of insolvency should unexpected personal expenses arise, but will enable you to buy bargains in a big way when they become truly available.

But the "cash" you keep doesn't have to be literally dollar bills. With today's lofty interest rates, it is foolhardy to tuck currency "under the mattress." Money should be put to work efficiently. What you should hold, then, are cash-equivalents—something that can be readily converted into cash on an instant's notice. Thus, you should use income-producing vehicles that are immune to anything more than minimal price fluctuation and have an active and liquid market.

Most Americans seeking both liquidity and current income habitually deposit their idle cash in a savings account. That makes reasonably good sense. Although some institutions could impose a short waiting period in a crunch situation, most deposits can be withdrawn any time at will. And deposits of up to $100,000 per account are covered by federal insurance programs. (I'll discuss the adequacy of these programs later in this chapter.)

Unfortunately, the interest these accounts pay is quite low compared to what's available elsewhere in the money market. The maximum returns savings institutions are allowed to pay have been limited by law. This situation is being corrected. The Depository Institutions Deregulation and Monetary Control Act of 1980, which became effective in October of that year, has paved the way for the removal of such interest ceilings. But the phase-in process will take six years, so rates from savings accounts won't be fully competitive until the latter part of the 1980s.

Other Americans have been switching their money into six-month savings certificates which provide much higher income. They, too, are reasonably safe. The drawback here is that the saver must pay a fairly large penalty should he find it necessary to redeem the certificates for cash before the six-month holding period is up.

Thus, starting in the late 1970s, more and more people have turned to the so-called money market funds, which offer not only current income closely in line with the prevailing market rates, but instant redemption privileges as well. As a result, this new industry has enjoyed supergrowth; by the summer of 1980, it already had total assets of well over $80 billion. Unfortunately, investments in most of these funds will prove highly risky in the financial scenario I foresee.

At first glance, one can hardly find fault with these funds. They invest mainly in short-maturity papers issued by reputable banks and large corporations. But in the coming liquidity squeeze when bankruptcies proliferate, some banks and corporations will inevitably fail. Their papers could become worthless. And money-market fund holders, who are not protected by any of the federal insurance programs, will be indirectly hurt.

The mere suggestion that some banks may at some point find themselves insolvent is at odds with the consensus. The conventional wisdom holds that only irresponsible alarmists would question the safety of the banking system. Indeed, history is on the optimist's side. Since 1934, losses to bank depositors have been minimal despite the failure in recent years of such large banks as the Franklin National Bank and the United States National Bank.

But then, since the early 1930s, the banking industry has never been put to a real liquidity test. Loan losses have never been large enough to worry depositors. Henceforth, however, things won't run quite so smoothly.

At the heart of the problem is the overextended condition of the entire system. Currently, for example, loans extended by commercial banks are equivalent to more than 80% of their deposits. This means that, for every dollar on deposit with a commercial bank, there is less than 20¢ in cash, investments, and other assets to cover its potential withdrawal. And of that small amount, nearly two-thirds is represented by fixed assets like buildings and equipment and by investments in state and local government securities. In a liquidity squeeze, these investments could hardly be liquidated in a hurry.

The balance is in cash, deposits at Federal Reserve Banks, and, to a great extent, U.S. government securities. But bond prices have dropped so much in recent years that if Treasury holdings must be sold to raise cash, the banks would have to realize enormous capital losses. These holdings are currently carried on the books at cost.

To be sure, if everything is moving along smoothly, and if nothing comes along to rock the financial boat, there would be little to worry about. Deposit withdrawals wouldn't show unusual increases. But the trouble now is that many of the currently outstanding bank loans are sure to turn sour in the difficult times ahead.

On a worldwide basis, the weakest link in the banking chain is the mountain of debt owed by the less developed countries (LDCs). At mid-1980, it totaled well over $400 billion. Many of these loans are already technically in default. The lenders merely consider them non-income-producing assets, hoping that somehow a new business boom will eventually revitalize the financial well-being of the countries involved. But that's whistling in the dark. Fortunately, a good deal of the total loans are owned by Eurodollar and other foreign banks. But the risk exposure to U.S. institutions alone is still estimated to exceed $100 billion.

The fact is, the LDCs have already been hurt badly in recent years by the soaring cost of energy; many are also being run by inept government leaders. They now depend on exports of raw materials to industrialized countries just to generate enough foreign exchange to pay interest on their debts. A depression in the U.S. and Europe—their principal markets—is bound to put them into serious insolvency. At some point, an across-the-board debt moratorium may become necessary. The victims will be major lending institutions.

Heavy losses are also in prospect in the area of personal loans. For the banks, this has always been the market in which the profit margin is the highest; so, therefore, are the risks involved. Aggravating the situation is the fact that the industry has in recent years significantly lowered minimum requirements to promote such loans, and has added further to its risk exposure as a result.

In the coming depression, there's no question that many of the personal loans secured by marginal borrowers will not be repaid.

Even more worrisome, as far as domestic lending is concerned, is the huge pile of real estate loans now outstanding. As I pointed out in the preceding chapter, mortgage delinquencies have already been rising rapidly and are higher now than any time since the Great Depression. Even government guarantees won't help the lenders much. FHA- and VA-insured mortgages represent only 6% of the total real estate loans held by the commercial banking system, and 7½% of those held by savings and loan associations.

Commercial and industrial loans, of course, are another potential source of the problem. This is especially so since an increasing proportion of them are now owed by secondary firms. Many prime corporations have made good progress in recent years toward securing long-term capital to replace short-term bank borrowings. The average quality of banks' loan portfolios has thus deteriorated.

True, some large companies may yet get help from the government. But don't expect Washington to bail out the tens of thousands of smaller companies which individually have little voting clout, but which together owe the majority of business loans outstanding. The fact that even as Chrysler was being bailed out by Washington in 1979–80 hundreds of its dealers went into bankruptcy underscores this point well.

Remember, almost all of the money lent by banks comes from depositors. When loan losses are heavy, some depositors have to be hurt. And this is where the Federal Deposit Insurance Corporation and the Federal Savings & Loans Insurance Corporation come in. They will help protect accounts having $100,000 or less.

To be sure, some alarmists even doubt that. Noting that the current FDIC insurance fund amounts to less than 1% of the insured deposits at commercial banks and that the FSLIC reserves are equivalent to only slightly more

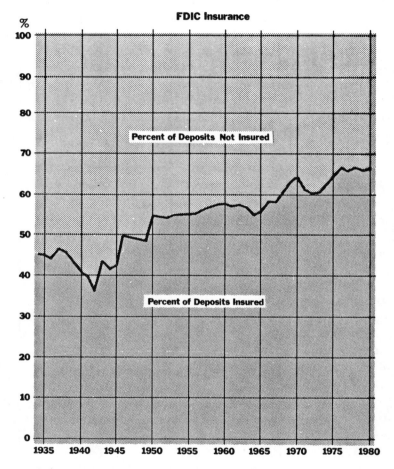

FDIC Insurance

Percent of Deposits Not Insured

Percent of Deposits Insured

If the assets of insolvent banks have to be liquidated hurriedly, the cash generated won't come anywhere near the amounts carried on the books. Fortunately, only about two-thirds of bank deposits are insured by federal agencies. Thus, while these deposits will be protected, holders of non-insured certificates of deposit will have to take the loss.

than 1% of all insured accounts at savings and loan associations, they foresee a total collapse of the banking system and advise Americans to head for the hills with cans of K-rations and a supply of shotguns and ammunition.

But those fears are exaggerated. The fact is, the insurance reserves of the FDIC and FSLIC do not by any means constitute all the monies available to pay off deposits. Those agencies have the authority to take over and sell the failing banks' assets. Proceeds received would then provide added funds to cover insured deposits.

The FDIC and FSLIC are also authorized to assist financially in the absorption of insured banks in difficulty by other insured banks. And they are allowed to purchase the assets or grant loans secured by the assets of the distressed banks. Indeed, in the largest insured bank failure since 1934, that of the Franklin National Bank, the FDIC provided enough assistance to enable other banks to assume virtually all of Franklin's deposit liabilities.

Admittedly, the sale of insolvent banks' assets usually won't fetch anywhere near the amounts carried on the books. But currently insured deposits account for only about 60% of all deposits, and only 50% of total bank assets. Thus, as long as the liquidation generates 50¢ for each dollar of bank assets, which is likely, the insured depositors are protected, though some delay in payment cannot be ruled out. Hence, large depositors, as well as banks' stockholders, will really be the principal and permanent victims.

Letting large depositors shoulder potential bank losses is in fact the very philosophy behind the government insurance program. Supposedly, large depositors such as rich individuals and prime corporations can better afford to take the beating. As long as smaller depositors are sheltered, the kind of total devastation that hit the banking system in the early 1930s won't recur.

Nevertheless, among today's large depositors are those mushrooming money market funds. This industry has, in effect, been pooling small savers' money to buy bank certificates of deposit (CDs). Thus, small investors putting money into these "liquid asset" funds are assuming much more risk than they realize.

To be sure, any massive problem confronting the banking system will probably be preceded by news of heavy loan losses. The more nimble saver could still avoid being hurt if he acts immediately to liquidate his money-market fund holdings. Thus, only those who don't keep abreast of financial developments will be badly hurt.

Unfortunately, most individuals just don't have the time or the required information to keep abreast of banking developments. That's why, for most investors in the early 1980s, I highly recommend Treasury bills for high income, safety, and liquidity.

From a credit standpoint, the obligations of the U.S. government, backed as they are by awesome federal taxing powers, are tops on any list of debt instruments. And Treasury bills are the most popular in the short-term money market. Among their chief advantages is liquidity. The vast secondary market for such paper virtually assures that sale or purchase in any amount can be handled with ease in the course of any business day.

New Treasury bills are issued regularly every week, and they come in denominations of $10,000 or more. As a rule, they mature three or six months from the date of issue, although bills with up to one-year maturities are becoming more and more available.

There's no indication on the bill itself showing how much interest is to be paid. The investor purchases a discounted security (at a price below face value) and the difference between the price paid and the bill's face value constitutes his interest income. Thus, the effective yield at the time of purchase is realized at maturity, regardless of interim market fluctuations. To assure maximum liquidity, I suggest you buy 90-day bills, and "roll them over" into new bills as they mature.

For a small fee, most brokers and banks will help you buy newly issued Treasury bills by submitting "non-competitive" bids at the Treasury's regular auctions. (For that matter, they can also buy and sell outstanding bills in the secondary market for you.) In agreeing to purchase bills at the weighted average price, these bids are always filled first. Since the professionals—banks, securities dealers, institutions, and related interests—generally oversubscribe new issues, private individuals thus enjoy a distinct edge, knowing in advance that their offers to purchase will be preferentially treated.

Bills purchased through a bank are carried as book entry items at the bank. Under rules set up by the Federal Reserve, the individual buyer is protected since the bank acts solely as custodian. But in the *extreme* event that a bank totally fails, there could be some delay before the individual gets his money. That's because while the Treasury acknowledges an obligation to the bank, the latter does not acknowledge a direct obligation to you.

To get around this problem—if you really question the soundness of your bank—purchase may be effected directly through the Treasury. In this case, the bills are held in the form of entries in accounts maintained by the Bureau of Public Debt. These bills must be transferred to a bank account if the individual wishes to sell before maturity. But this is a small inconvenience compared to the additional safety gained. The further advantage is that the Treasury acknowledges a direct obligation to you.

Bills to be held in a Treasury book-entry account may be purchased, without a maintenance charge, by submitting a tender to a Federal Reserve Bank or Branch or to the Bureau of Public Debt, Securities Transaction Branch, Washington, D.C. 20026. Tender forms may be obtained by writing to the Federal Reserve or the Bureau of Public Debt.

As noted earlier, T-bills are issued at a minimum denomination of $10,000. If you have less than that amount to invest, but seek higher-than-passbook interest income, I suggest you consider the securities of the Federal Land Bank.

The FLB is a federal agency that makes long-term, low-interest mortgage loans to farmers. To raise the necessary funds, it regularly sells to the public its own securities, some of which have short maturities. These securities are not the direct obligation of the U.S. government, but like those of a few other federal agencies, they are the second safest. All these agencies were established by acts of Congress; the government has an active interest in them through equity positions and supervisory controls.

For your purpose, though, the Federal Land Bank is the only one that has actively traded securities in denominations as low as $1,000. Again, for a fee, your broker can buy new issues in the secondary market. Depending on your broker or bank, the fee charged can sometimes be large enough to reduce your current yield, particularly if the transaction is relatively small. But if you are worried about a major credit crunch, sacrificing a little income to ensure top liquidity could help you sleep a lot better when the crisis arises.

CHAPTER FIFTEEN

Fixed-Income Securities

Once the liquidity squeeze has run its full course—that is, once marginal debtors have gone bankrupt in droves—demand for credit will soften and interest rates will then start declining. That will be the time for you to mobilize some of your cash reserves to lock in the lush yields available from long-term fixed-income securities. As interest rates drop, these investments in fixed-income issues will also appreciate in value. Thus, you'll have the best of both worlds.

Government and corporate bonds are, of course, the most important kind of fixed-income securities. Unlike stock quotations, their prices respond much more to changes in interest rate trends than to corporate developments.

Bond prices and bond yields typically move in opposite directions. Note that since the mid-1940s, when credit started expanding, interest rates have trended generally upward. As a result, bond prices have dropped over 60%. Significantly, interest rates also rose and hence bond prices dropped between 1928 and 1932, when a liquidity squeeze unfolded. It's a timely reminder that buying bonds just because the economy has started to soften is premature and can be terribly costly.

On the other hand, between 1932 and 1946, bond yields declined without any interruption. Over the same period, bond prices, as measured by Standard & Poor's High-Grade Corporate Bond Index, rose from around 75 to 123, a gain of nearly 65%.

As I noted before, when the coming liquidity squeeze reaches its climax, you won't miss it. So, there's no need for you to decide beforehand just when to start buying bonds. It's never too early, however, for you to start familiarizing yourself with this important investment vehicle. Later this decade, it will offer many handsome profit opportunities.

A bond is essentially a long-term IOU. When a new bond is offered, the issuer is in effect borrowing money on certain specified terms from the buyer, who agrees to those terms. A mortgage bond is a security secured by a collateral such as real estate property or equipment. When the bond is backed solely by the issuer's general credit, with no lien on specific assets, it is called a debenture.

While a shareholder in a corporation is a part owner, the bondholder is simply a creditor. As a result, he does not share in future growth of the corporation; but neither does he assume the full risk of earnings declines and dividend cuts. And should the company become insolvent, the bond buyer has prior claim on assets over the common shareholder.

The exact terms of a bond issue—interest rate, maturity date, rights in case of default, and so on—are always spelled out in detail in the indenture executed before the issue is offered for sale. But just as shareholders do not always have to read the bylaws and certificates of incorporation for the companies they partially own, bond buyers do not neces-

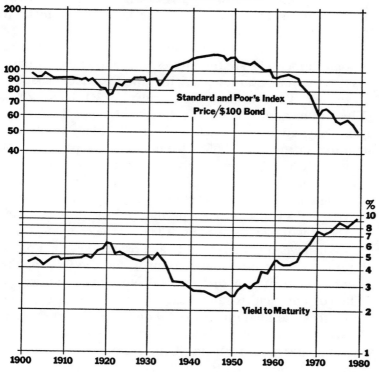

High Grade Corporate Bonds

Standard and Poor's Index
Price/$100 Bond

Yield to Maturity

Once the coming liquidity squeeze has climaxed, long-term interest rates should start declining. The drop may not be as steep as that occurring between 1920 and 1945. Even so, a period of rising bond prices can reasonably be expected. Only quality issues, however, should be considered.

sarily have to be familiar with all the fine print in the indenture—especially if they restrict their holdings to high-grade issues.

Most bonds are rated by independent organizations like Moody's and Standard & Poor's. These rating services assess risks against earning power, resources, capital structure, and property protection. Moody's ratings, for example, range from Aaa, Aa, and A down through C. In the 1980s, I think it's advisable for the lay investor to limit himself to triple-A issues.

For an investor, the two most important provisions of a bond's indenture are the interest rate and maturity date. As a matter of fact, these data are how a particular issue is identified. Take a listing that reads: AT&T 8.80s, 2005. This just means the bond was issued by the telephone company, pays an annual interest of 8.80% of face value, and matures in the year 2005. All bonds have a par value of $1,000 (although they are always quoted with 100 being par). Thus the holder of one of these bonds—regardless of his original cost or the current quotation—is assured of receiving $88 a year in interest payments through 2005, when the bond will be redeemed at $1,000 by the company.

Whenever a bond is bought at a price other than par, a built-in capital gain (or loss) is involved. And figuring the yield to maturity for such a bond is mildly complicated. The current yield is calculated the same way as for common stocks: annual interest is divided by the market price. However, since a bond is to be redeemed at par when it matures, it's more realistic—if the security is selling at a discount (below par)—to add to the current yield the pro rata annual capital appreciation in prospect.

To demonstrate, let's take an 8.25% bond maturing in exactly ten years that is currently selling at 80 ($800 per bond). Since the bond pays an annual interest of $82.50, its *current yield* is $82.50 divided by $800—or 10.3%. The bondholder, however, is also assured of a 20-point ($200) capital gain since he will receive $1,000 when the issue matures. Prorating this 25% appreciation over the life of the bond, and then adding it to the current yield, will give a *yield to maturity* of 11.7%. (Compound interest is involved in this calculation; such figures are published in yield tables available at most brokerage offices.)

On the other hand, if a bond is selling at a premium over par, it has a built-in *depreciation to maturity*. In such a case, the yield to maturity will be lower than the current yield.

Since the prices of high-grade bonds are largely determined by prevailing interest-rate changes—and not by developments peculiar to individual companies—an actively traded bond is seldom much overpriced or underpriced at any given time. The efficient bond market has a way of evening things out. For that reason, even the private investor who has no bond-buying experience should have little difficulty buying what he selects at a fair market price.

By far the safest fixed-income securities are Treasury notes and bonds. Like Treasury bills, they are backed by the full taxing power of the government. Notes have maturities up to seven years, while bonds have original maturities of five years and longer. Both trade over the counter, and are generally quoted in terms of 32nds. Thus, a price quotation of 93.8 (or 93-8) means $93\frac{8}{32}$ or $93\frac{1}{4}$. Since bonds are quoted with 100 as par, that 93-8 quote means $932.50 per $1,000 bond. Incidentally, the settlement day for government securities transactions is usually the next full business day following the trade.

As far as private investors are concerned, Treasury notes and bonds are not significantly different. In fact, the *Wall Street Journal* and other dailies usually list quotations of these issues in the same table.

Treasury notes and bonds are available in registered

as well as in coupon form. In the case of a registered issue, the name and address of the owner are recorded with the government. This form of ownership is relatively safer against theft, and interest payments are mailed directly to the owner. A coupon bond, on the other hand, is technically owned by the bearer, whoever he may be. To get his interest payments, which are usually payable semiannually, the holder has to cut a coupon off from the bond certificate and redeem it at a bank. Coupon bonds are more suitable for large institutional investors.

Registered and coupon bonds are interchangeable. But the Treasury Department closes its books for the transfer of registered bonds one month prior to each interest payment date.

Treasury notes are generally non-callable. In other words, they cannot be redeemed at the government's option prior to maturity. For high coupon issues, this is an important feature. Even if interest rates drop a few percentage points in the ensuing years, the Treasury cannot recall these notes and replace them with new ones that carry lower interest coupons.

Some long-term bonds, however, can be called for redemption at par a few years before they reach maturity. But in the 1980s this call feature will by and large be quite meaningless. Most callable bonds are now and will be selling at large discounts from their face value. Until long-term interest rates have dropped sharply, there is no reason whatsoever why the government would want to retire these bond issues prematurely.

As I noted in the chapter on short-term paper, a number of federal agencies are also authorized to sell debt to the investing public. Many of their securities have both long and short maturities. While they are not the direct obligations of the U.S. government, they're the next best thing to Treasury securities. Reflecting the slightly greater risks involved, the agency issues generally offer somewhat higher returns than Treasury securities. Daily quotations of these issues are published in the *Wall Street Journal* under the heading: "Government, Agency, and Miscellaneous Securities." Listed in approximate order of size, here are some of the more important agencies:

Federal Home Loan Bank . . . organized to extend to residential mortgage-lending and thrift institutions, such as savings and loan associations.

Federal Land Banks . . . a twelve-institution system that makes long-term, low-interest mortgage loans to farmers through various associations.

Federal Intermediate Credit Banks . . . underwriters of the seasonal needs of farmers and stockmen in the areas of production and marketing by discounting agricultural loan paper.

Central Bank for Cooperatives . . . assists agricultural associations by making loans on commodity crops, property, equipment, and facilities.

International Bank for Reconstruction & Development (World Bank) . . . organized at the Bretton Woods Conference in 1944 to stimulate investment in war-devastated or emerging nations.

Even after the liquidity squeeze is over and interest rates have started declining, the economy is likely to keep contracting for years. For that reason, I advise you to *stay away from municipal bonds.*

In all fairness, I must note that as the 1980s began, New York and a number of other major cities seemed to have survived their earlier flirtations with bankruptcy, and most state and local governments had managed to report fiscal surpluses. Moreover, by mid-1980, interest rates of new municipal issues were topping 10%. As always, the interest paid on municipals is exempt from federal income taxes and, in some cases, from state or local levies as well. One doesn't have to be in a high tax bracket to be tempted by these generous yields.

Nevertheless, although they are considered "government" bonds, municipal issues are nowhere as safe as U.S. Treasury issues. Although so far there have been relatively few instances in which a state or a city was unable to make good its general obligation debts, such cases are by no means unheard of. In the economic chaos of the 1930s, over 2,000 communities and local governments defaulted when the time came to pay their debts. And as recently as 1970, one federal court approved a plan whereby Saluda, N.C., bondholders would be paid off at the rate of only 41¢ on the dollar.

Particularly disturbing, meanwhile, is the fact that most city and state treasurers will find themselves in a more illiquid position during the 1980s than the 1930s. Their tax revenues will be much depressed by the ebbing economy. Budget surpluses can vanish quickly in the face of continuing spending increases, particularly pension and unemployment obligations.

Time was when state and local taxes were of only small concern to the public. Governors and mayors seldom had any trouble pushing through tax increases, wherever necessary. Not so in recent years. Proposition 13s have brought a nationwide taxpayers' revolt to the fore. Meanwhile, many municipalities already cut their budgets close to the bone in the 1970s. There may not be sufficient fat that can be trimmed to help offset ever-rising outlays. In short, their ability to service municipal debt will be sorely tested in the years immediately ahead. I wouldn't be surprised if many fail the test.

If you must have a higher interest income than what's available from Treasury or federal agency issues and are willing to accept a little more market risk, I think you'd be better off buying top-rated corporate bonds. No matter how well a municipality manages its finances, it still cannot raise revenues much, if at all, in a shrinking economy. In such an economy, it'll probably operate in the red.

Industry will suffer from a profit squeeze, too. But a well-managed corporation, by way of contrast, could and should continue to earn at least enough profits to fulfill its long-term obligations. Back in the 1930s, high-grade corporate bonds were among the most rewarding investments available.

For that matter, you should also consider the preferred stock of top corporations. Unlike bonds, preferred stocks do not have a maturity date and their holders are not creditors of the issuing corporations. As such, they involve more risk than debt securities. But if you select only companies that boast superior financial strength, the fact that these issues will never mature can be a plus. In a period of declining interest rates, buying sound preferred stocks enables you to enjoy their lush income *indefinitely*. For that reason, these issues could appreciate in value even more rapidly than bonds offering the same current return.

What about convertible debentures? They are corporate debt issues which can be converted into common stocks at a specific price, but which nevertheless pay a fixed interest rate, mature on a specified date, and are senior to common stock; they also provide bondlike protection on the downside. Theoretically, when interest rates start declining, and when the stocks have completed their bear market, these securities should be the ideal investment vehicle.

The unfortunate fact of the matter is that there is no such thing as an ideal security. And there's no way an investor can enjoy all the theoretical advantages of convertible issues without giving up something.

For one thing, at the bottom of a protracted bear market, the conversion rates of most debentures will no doubt be far above the depressed market price of their underlying stocks. Hence, the conversion feature would be quite academic. Still, because of this feature, the convertibles are likely to offer a lower interest return than straight bonds of comparable quality.

Speaking of quality, convertibles are usually issued only by firms which have to offer prospective buyers a "sweetener" because they have trouble selling a simple bond to begin with. In other words, the issuers are probably secondary companies with less-than-healthy balance sheets. In the economic environment I foresee for the 1980s, investments in such firms are decidedly not advisable.

Actually, for the venturesome who want to capitalize on a downtrend in interest rates, I recommend the purchase of long-term government bonds *on margin*. Margin requirements for buying and carrying Treasury securities are not subject to limits imposed by the Federal Reserve Board. And most brokerage firms are willing to lend you as much as 90% of the purchase price. But to avoid your being upset by any interim reverses, I suggest you borrow only 75%.

Such a "conservative speculation" can be highly rewarding. First, you should be able to enjoy very generous income. Once the interest rates in general start to trend decidedly downward, short-term rates are bound to be much lower than long-term rates. Thus, even though you have to pay interest on the margin debt, your bond will provide you with more than enough income to bring net yield sky-high. Moreover, the margin transaction will also leverage your capital appreciation sharply upward.

Here's a hypothetical situation: let's say long-term government bonds are currently yielding 10%, so that a twenty-year issue with an 8% coupon is selling at around 82¾. If you buy $10,000 face value worth, the total cost would be $8,275. Since you borrow 75%, or $6,206, you have to put up only $2,069. From these bonds you will receive an annual interest income of $800 (8% of $10,000 face value). Now with short-term rates much lower, your brokerage firm will probably charge you, say, only 6% on the margin debt, or $372. Your net current income: $800 — $372 = $428. Remember you originally put up only $2,069. That $428 income would thus be equivalent to a yield of over 20% annually.

Let's suppose further that long-term rates drop three percentage points in a couple of years or so. Now, that 8% issue can be sold at 110.55 for $11,055. After repaying the broker for the $6,206 margin loan, your net proceeds will equal $4,849. This represents a capital appreciation on your original investment of $2,069 of nearly 135%!

Leverage works, of course, both ways. So, don't play this game until the liquidity crisis has climaxed. But if you have done your homework and are convinced that economic conditions are such that money must get cheaper and cheaper, I think you will agree that using Treasury bonds in this manner is far more rewarding than gambling in most other markets.

CHAPTER SIXTEEN

The Stock Market in Perspective

In the early chapters of this book, where I discussed the correlation between the behavior of various investment markets and the long-term credit cycle in the past, I pointed out that the stock market by and large did very well during periods of orderly credit expansion, but did poorly in periods of credit *contraction* as well as *excessive* credit *expansion*.

Thus, between 1929 and the early 1940s, when debt liquidation was in progress, stock prices showed a net decline of some 75%. In the quarter century thereafter, when credit expansion proceeded orderly, the strongest and longest bull market on record took place. The Dow Jones industrials multiplied more than ten times—catapulting from a low of 88 in 1942 to nearly 1,000 in 1968. From then on, credit expansion became excessive and debt explosion eventually brought about double-digit inflation, and the stock market weakened in response.

The inferior performance of the stock market during the 1970s, to be sure, was nowhere as conspicuous as that of the 1930s. But the damage was almost as serious. Adjusted for inflation, the Dow Jones Industrial Average actually lost, between the late 1960s and the start of the 1980s, more than 60% of its value. Worse yet, throughout that period, the current income provided by dividends was far less than that available from most other investments. This added insult to injury.

Even so, the stock market is likely to continue acting poorly at least in the early part of the 1980s. Reason: the current decade will be characterized by debt liquidation.

My expectation of declining stock prices in the years ahead is, of course, at odds with the prevailing consensus. Wall Street experts have lately been saying that the 1980s will be "the decade of the common stocks." To them, the fact that stock prices (in current dollars) have moved sideways for over a dozen years while corporate profits have soared means that equities are underpriced.

Actually, while stocks look cheap, they really aren't. I will discuss this point in more detail in the next chapter, where I'll also tell you when real bargains are likely to be available. In the meantime, I think it's important to identify first the key factors which govern the market's underlying trend. Only by recognizing these factors can one anticipate future market movements with confidence.

Most people still think that stock prices are directly determined by the level of company earnings. But the market's behavior since the late 1960s belies that argument. Between 1967 and 1979, corporate profits jumped 170% from $44.8 billion to $121.5 billion, but the market didn't go up. Other experts suggest that the interest rate trend has a more important influence on the market. A rise in the cost of money, they say, hurt stock prices, and vice versa. But then, the great postwar bull market I mentioned earlier took place in the face of rising interest rates. Long-term Treasury bond yields, for instance, were only about 2½% in the early and mid-1940s; they were close to 6% by the late 1960s. In other words, during the quarter century when stocks skyrocketed, the cost of capital actually climbed well over 100%.

When you come right down to it, one can make only this statement about the market without equivocation: stock prices respond to changes in the demand for and the supply of the shares involved. To be sure, the changes are influenced by a great variety of complex factors, which include ever-changing economic, monetary, and psychological developments. But that statement does point up the simple fact that the key to determining the future market trend is to find out how the potential supply and demand shape up.

Actually there are different kinds of supply and demand, and their interaction, in turn, determines the duration of various market trends. For instance, week-to-week and day-to-day market moves are largely influenced by the supply and demand forces generated by in-and-out traders. Most such market players base their decisions on technical considerations like chart formations and trend lines. Others react to late-breaking news. It is difficult for the average private investor to move in and out as nimbly as an active trader must. Trying to trade on such short-term movements is thus tantamount to speculating on random fluctuations, which is more rewarding to brokers than to investors.

On the other hand, long-term (primary) market trends, which typically last for several years or decades, can be predicted with a high degree of accuracy. They are directly related to the supply and demand forces coming from long-term private investors, which, in turn, are governed by the availability of investment funds and the public's confidence in the nation's economic future.

In between the two are intermediate (secondary) trends, which usually last for several months or occasionally, up to a couple of years. They are influenced by changes in the supply and demand associated with veteran and professional investors, who control the relatively more mobile investment funds. The amount of money they decide to put into or take out of the equity market is often correlated to economic and monetary developments.

To be more specific, a *primary* bull market typically results when an increasing number of long-term individual investors, helped by rising savings and confidence, buy and stash away common stocks and mutual fund shares. Their accumulation not only injects capital into the stock market, but brings about a gradual attrition of the active supply of equities as well. Hence, stock prices trend upward.

Conversely, when these investors run out of investment funds, lose their confidence, or find more attractive investment vehicles elsewhere, they gradually sell more stocks than they buy. Such net liquidation by long-term investors drains money from the market and also effects an increase in the active supply. A *primary* bear market is then launched.

By way of comparison, a *secondary* bull market (which may occur in the midst of a primary bear market, as well as a primary bull market) emerges when there's an influx of mobile investment funds coming from the comparatively more active investors and traders—who can run the gamut from well-informed institutional professionals to ill-advised dabblers. The astute ones in this group usually act to anticipate a cyclical economic expansion, while the inexperienced react to it. By the same token, a *secondary* bear market is caused by an exodus of such mobile investment funds, in anticipation of and later in response to a cyclical recession. Proceeds from such sales, unlike those resulting from long-term liquidation, will more often than not return to the market once economic prospects improve.

Since secondary market trends are associated with

changing economic and monetary conditions, it is important to keep abreast of developments in these areas if you want to capitalize on these trends. But remember, you'll be competing with veteran and substantial investors who spend full time at it. So, unless you do your homework, you'll have the odds working against you. In this regard, getting proper professional help of your own could often spell the difference between profits and losses.

Once you are able to identify and anticipate secondary trends, you can, of course, decide when to buy and sell stocks. However, it is virtually impossible even for the professionals to anticipate every secondary market swing correctly. The non-veteran investor is thus better off concentrating on riding on the primary trend. Even if he fails to anticipate a secondary bear market in the midst of a primary bull market, for example, he could still come out ahead by just "sitting tight."

The market performance of the early 1960s is a good case history. In 1962, the economy was expanding healthily and the monetary climate was stable and bright. And in John F. Kennedy, Americans had a young and energetic president to give them confidence. But suddenly that spring, the market "fell out of bed." Between March 15 and June 26, the Dow average tumbled a solid 26%, from 723.54 to 535.76. While many of the uninformed literally panicked, the cool-headed merely stayed put. By the following spring, all their paper losses had been recouped. And a few years later, the average was a whole lot higher.

Fortunately, it is not too difficult to identify an ongoing primary trend. As noted at the outset, these trends are directly related to the supply and demand force generated by long-term private investors. History shows that this group doesn't change its investment attitude abruptly or drastically. The thing to do, then, is to find out how these investors have been behaving of late and what the recent trend has been.

In this regard, the flow-of-funds account prepared by the Federal Reserve Board is particularly helpful. Among other things, the data include the net purchases or net sales of corporate stocks and mutual fund shares by "households" on a quarterly basis.

These FRB figures go only as far back as 1946, but the history is more than long enough to be informative. It's no coincidence, for example, that in the late 1940s and throughout the 1950s, when the market was pushing firmly upward, private Americans were consistently putting money into the equity market. They thereby generated a constant and powerful demand force and reduced the floating supply at the same time.

In 1959, these individuals for the first time sold more corporate stocks than they bought, but they did invest heavily in mutual fund shares. So, on balance, they remained a demand force, injecting some $600 million of new savings into the equity market. But in 1960, net liquidation of corporate stocks finally exceeded purchases of mutual funds. Meaning: long-term investors started becoming a supply factor on balance. Together with corporations, which continually add to the supply through new stock offerings, they began draining money from the marketplace.

During the early 1960s, while the economy was still expanding nicely, private long-term investors kept withdrawing dollars from the equity market. Stock prices managed to stay reasonably firm, however. Accumulation by financial institutions (pension funds and insurance companies, for example) and speculative traders served to offset the withdrawal. But by the mid-1960s the market began to feel the effect of the long-term liquidation. The Dow

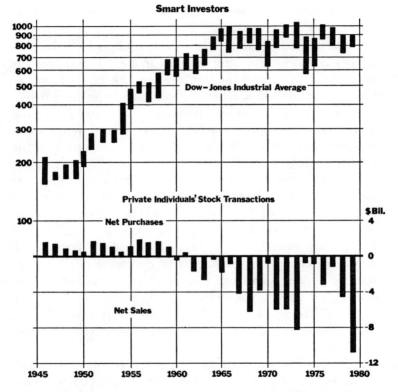

Smart Investors

Dow–Jones Industrial Average

Private Individuals' Stock Transactions

$Bil.

Net Purchases

Net Sales

Private investors, as distinguished from financial institutions, have a remarkable record of having bought low and sold high. In the late 1940s through the 1950s, a period when stock prices multiplied manyfold, they were persistently net buyers. Over the past fifteen years, when stock prices have moved sideways even in the face of accelerating inflation, they have sold stocks heavily on balance.

average, after having approached the 1,000 level for the first time ever in January 1966, tumbled sharply thereafter; it fell below 750 by October of that year.

The market recovered in 1967–68, but has since been unable to do any better than just moving sideways, even as inflation sent the prices of goods and services soaring across the board.

It's perhaps appropriate to note at this point that financial institutions never put much money in stocks during the 1940s and 1950s, when equities were cheap and rising. Instead, they started to buy stocks heavily in the late 1960s, just when the quarter-century primary bull market was reaching its climax. Thus, unlike private individuals, they have the "distinguished" record of having bought stocks timidly when prices were low and boldly when prices were high. This should put to rest once and for all one of Wall Street's most enduring myths, which suggests that professional traders and money managers represent "smart" money, while small private investors represent something less than that.

Why have private investors been able to chalk up such a commendable record, while the pros have had a hard time just catching up with the averages? No, it's not that the investing public is necessarily that much smarter. But collectively, they represent the most powerful market force. The fact is, private individuals have long held and still hold by far the largest block of stocks—for that matter, they also own the bulk of the nation's financial assets.

By way of contrast, even though professional money managers are active in the market, ever-churning the portfolios of their institutional clients, they are limited by the amount of new money available for investment. Hence, their transactions tend to affect the market only temporarily.

When it comes to the long-term supply and demand,

there's no question that private investors collectively call the shots. This is what the free-market system is all about.

Though largely on the sell side of late, private individuals have nevertheless retained their investing flexibility. In the past decade and a half, for instance, they reduced their net liquidation markedly on three occasions—in late 1966, 1970, and late 1974. Those were the periods when the market registered the three major bottoms of the past fifteen years.

If nothing else, this reveals that most long-term investors are "price elastic"—that is, their demand increases when prices decline, and vice versa. Unlike traders and even money managers, who often buy in euphoric times and sell in panic, private individuals cool-headedly buy stocks only when equities are conspicuously cheap and sell when they are distinctly dear. This goes a long way toward explaining why private investors bought stocks on balance in the 1940s and 1950s and sold in the 1960s and 1970s.

Another reason for the switch from being net buyers to net sellers has been the confidence factor. Various public opinion polls have revealed that immediately after World War II, Americans all looked forward to a brand new era of prosperity. The U.S. had just proven itself to be the strongest country in the world—both economically and militarily. In the 1960s, however, confidence started to wane. And more recently, it has sunk to an all-time low. At the start of the 1980s, a majority of Americans actually believed for the first time since the 1930s that a "depression" was around the corner.

Confidence, of course, is an intangible, resulting from a variety of inputs. All economic, social, and political developments at home and abroad have something to do with it. But one thing, I submit, plays a more important role than anything else. And it is the financial well-being of the average American. When a person has lots of money in the bank, he is bound to be quite optimistic about the future. But when he is laden with debt and has trouble making ends meet, no amount of bullish forecasts can make him feel truly confident.

The financial well-being of all Americans is, of course, reflected in the condition of their collective balance sheet. The ratio of total liabilities to total liquid assets is most significant in this regard. And that goes back to the loan-to-deposit ratio I discussed earlier in this book. All this explains why the long-term credit cycle has so much to do with the stock market's primary trend.

Since the nation is now in the process of shifting from excessive credit expansion to credit contraction, which will involve many bankruptcies, public confidence is not likely to show any dramatic improvement any time soon. On top of that, the sluggish economy I foresee for at least the early 1980s is not likely to generate too much excess money for most middle-income Americans. Hence, private households, which sold a record $11.9 billion worth of equities as recently as 1979, will almost certainly keep on liquidating—perhaps even at an accelerated pace. And they can do so for a long, long time; their holdings at the start of the decade amounted to well over $600 billion.

Can financial institutions keep on buying enough to offset that liquidation? Hardly. The demographic changes that will take place in this decade and the economic slowdown in prospect both suggest that the net cash flow to pension and retirement funds will soon top out and then decline rapidly. Once the drop in inflation rates becomes conspicuous, money managers will find it more desirable to invest the bulk of their funds in fixed-income securities that offer yields well above the actuarial requirements of most trusts and which will appreciate in value as interest rates drop.

The upshot, therefore, is that the stock market will see

more supply than demand in the years ahead, and prices will trend downward as a result. In the next chapter, I'll suggest investment strategies to take advantage of this primary bear market and indicate when the next bull market is likely to begin.

CHAPTER SEVENTEEN

Riding the Stock Market Tide

There's no good reason why investors should be afraid of a primary bear market. Of course, you can no longer simply buy any stock and expect a rising market to drive its price up. And trading on "hot tips" and rumors will almost surely result in big losses. But bear markets do offer many extra profit opportunities that would not otherwise be available.

Take a hypothetical situation in which two investors are interested in a growth company whose stock is selling at 50. Having already risen sharply of late, the issue is overpriced. Investor A nevertheless rushes in to buy it immediately. But investor B decides to wait, anticipating the unfolding of a primary bear market. Suppose further that a protracted bear market does take place and that by the end of the market decline, the stock has dropped to 25. Investor B buys it at this point.

Note that with the same amount of money, B has now acquired twice as many shares as A. If the stock recovers to 40, B will have a 15-point gain, as against a 10-point loss for A. And if the stock rises further to 60, B will enjoy a 140% appreciation, seven times more than A's 20%.

Chances are, moreover, that investor A won't even hold the stock all the way through the decline and the subsequent run-up. As the bear market progresses, he no doubt becomes increasingly nervous, and quite likely he'll bail out in panic near 25. Even if he survives the decline, the break-even syndrome will probably prompt him to get out as soon as the stock approaches 50.

Though hypothetical, the above example is in fact a very common occurrence. And it goes to show that, although almost everyone can make money in a bull market, a bear market is what separates the informed investor from the lucky trader. To help you become an informed and successful investor in a primary bear market, here are a few useful guidelines.

• *Don't get attached to your equity holdings.* Holding on tightly to "good" stocks "for the long pull" is okay when a long-term bull market is in progress. But in a primary bear market, this sort of love affair will prove damaging to both your bank account and your peace of mind.

• *Don't expect those lofty quotations of the past to return.* Even investors who have every intention of liquidating unwanted stocks often fail to do so because they keep waiting for prices to return to the peaks reached during the height of the speculative spree. In all probability, those high levels will not be attained again in the 1980s.

• *Don't hold on to losers simply because you hate to take losses.* In the absence of an across-the-board and sustained market advance, inaction is not just impractical, it is demoralizing as well.

Look through a long-term chart book and you'll notice that any number of securities are now selling at levels well below where they were years ago. Many shareholders have undoubtedly held those issues all the way down, eternally hoping that "the worst is over and a recovery won't be far behind."

Had those shareholders liquidated their holdings years ago and put the capital to work more intelligently, they might well have experienced real recovery instead of continued capital attrition. To add insult to injury, every time they thought about their unfortunate investments during those years, they probably got a bad case of depression.

Thus, refusing to face up to the fact that the losses, whether taken or not, *already* exist, may actually endanger whatever capital is left. By contrast, once the loss is taken, you will be able to use that capital more gainfully elsewhere. As a bonus, you will also experience some psychological relief, and may even realize some tax benefits.

• *Don't, however, be obsessed with tax considerations.* One of the more common reasons why many long-term investors fail to realize gains is their reluctance to pay capital gains taxes. Important though they may be, tax considerations should never come before investment merits. It is often far cheaper to pay a tax on the capital gains only than to risk a much larger loss on total capital.

Actually, as soon as a stock advances from its purchase price, a potential tax liability accrues. It can be removed either by nailing down the profit and paying the taxes, or having the stock retreat to below the original purchase price, thereby eliminating the paper profit. Obviously, the first alternative is the more pleasant.

Another way of looking at the "frozen-in-by-taxes" situation is to consider the tax liability more or less as an interest-free margin loan from the Internal Revenue Service. While it is usually smart to be able to get interest-free loans, it is not advisable at all to use margin to buy stocks during a primary bear market.

• *Capitalize on technical rallies.* Even during major bear markets, there will be secondary advances that last a couple of months or longer. They afford excellent opportunities to move out of unwanted issues. This seems almost too elementary for me to state. However, many investors who intend to sell during the "next" rally often turn euphoric once the market stages a recovery. As a result, they miss the opportunity to sell at better prices.

• *Do some careful bargain hunting.* Even before the primary bear trend has run its course, occasionally panic selling waves are likely to render most stocks temporarily oversold. A recovery substantial enough to offer good profit opportunities with limited downside risks would then occur. That's when some of your carefully husbanded cash reserves can be put to use. The advent of such a recovery can only be detected, however, through careful analyses of market, economic, and monetary indicators. Seeking reliable professional help may therefore be necessary; otherwise, you'll be better off just sitting on the sideline. In any event, don't hold on to your new trading positions too long. Overstaying a technical rally is a very dangerous game. In the worst bear market of all times—the 1929–1932 one—the most staggering losses were incurred not in the initial crash, but during the two years after April 1930.

• *Sell institutional favorites short.* Selling short is just a simple reversal of the normal buy-and-then-sell sequence. When the initial short sale is made, the stock has to be borrowed from a third party so that delivery can be made to the investor who buys it from you. This borrowing process sounds complicated, but it is really a simple matter routinely handled by most brokerage firms through a few accounting entries. The short position is subsequently closed out, or "covered," when the stock involved is finally repurchased and returned to the lender.

In an advancing market, of course, selling short is highly risky. But in a long-term bear market, the opposite is true. As most stocks will be trending downward, the odds will be very much in your favor. Low-yield equities held heavily by financial institutions will be particularly vulnerable to undergoing steep nosedives. In the 1970s, they had been buoyed by persistent institutional accumulation. In the years ahead, many pension funds will find themselves with negative cash flow. Their attempt to liquidate overpriced stocks in a market with few large buyers around will surely result in large price declines.

To minimize your risk, allocate only a small portion of your capital to selling short at any one time.

• *Protect short positions with options.* Understandably, most investors are still afraid to sell stocks short outright. *Theoretically*, if things go wrong, losses can be unlimited. I think this fear is unwarranted. Still, you can easily limit your maximum risk nowadays by buying a call option on the stock shorted. A call entitles you to buy the stock at a specific price within a specific time.

Let's say you sell short 100 shares of XYZ at 50. If that stock drops to 30, you'll have a $2,000 profit. But if the stock should soar to 100, your losses would be $5,000! To hedge against such a catastrophe, buy a call on the stock entitling you to purchase the stock at, say 50 or 55. (The lower the call price, the more it'll cost you.) At any rate, having such an option would put a limit on your possible losses. What you pay will represent your insurance premium.

The coming primary bear market won't go on forever, of course. Sometime in the 1980s, stocks will become really cheap, and they should start trending upward thereafter. The key question, then, is how to tell when stocks are really underpriced.

One thing you shouldn't rely on is the price/earnings ratio. The P/E is the numerical relationship between a stock's current price and its annual earnings—and nothing more. As an investment guide, it is not much more useful than any other number from zero to infinity. Brokers and stock analysts rely heavily on it only because it is the handiest tool they can use to *rationalize* their recommendations.

Since the late 1960s, in fact, P/E ratios in general have been declining steadily. Because of that, Wall Street has insisted throughout the past dozen years that "stocks are cheap." But as it has turned out, they just got cheaper and cheaper.

The fact is, P/E ratios cannot substitute for investment judgment. And good judgment involves knowing what governs the demand for stocks. As I explained in the last chapter, stock prices are heavily influenced by investors' sentiment. And this important factor is not included in the earnings ratio whatsoever.

Moreover, P/E ratios are meaningless because the quality of earnings at individual companies often varies markedly. There have been efforts to standardize accounting procedures, but the bases on which reported profits are computed still differ from one company to another.

The variance sometimes reflects differences in the nature of the business of individual companies or industries. But there are also major disparities among companies' accounting practices relating to, for example, the treatment of depreciation, inventory, investment tax credits, research and development expenditures, and related items.

It is not uncommon, therefore, for a company following conservative accounting practices to write off all research and development expenses and make-ready costs and to use accelerated depreciation and amortization schedules to report much lower earnings than an identical firm that uses more liberal methods. Yet the first company, enjoying a larger cash flow because of smaller tax liabilities, would actually be in a better financial position to pay dividends and to work toward future growth.

The quality of reported earnings is also affected by the balance sheet. Though most Wall Street analysts scarcely discuss the financial position of companies they study, the capital structure of a corporation has a great bearing on the amount of earnings available for dividend payments or future expansion. For example, a company that is debt-heavy must allocate a substantial portion of future profits for repaying creditors, leaving less money available for payouts to common shareholders. For that reason, such earnings should not be capitalized as generously—at least by informed investors—as those of a debt-free concern.

How, then, can we tell when the primary bear market will finally be reversed? For one thing, investors' sentiment should improve and that should happen after the credit contraction process has restored financial liquidity to most households. To this end, keeping an eye on banking statistics should give you an early clue. A significant and sustained drop in the long-term interest rates would, for example, be promising.

For another, the flow of new money from private individuals into the stock market should increase significantly.

And that is likely to take place only when stock yields compare favorably with bond yields.

Many among the new breed of investors tend to ignore the relationship between stock and bond yields. Some even ridicule the theory that a meaningful relationship really exists. This cavalier attitude toward an important investment yardstick is partly understandable. Since the mid-1930s, the two yields have more often than not moved in opposite directions.

Still, the correlation between the stock market and the bond market should not be dismissed lightly. The fact remains that stocks and bonds are both investment media competing for capital, and funds do flow from one market to another.

To understand why the stock-and-bond-yield relationship has not really lost its validity permanently, it is necessary to recognize that the capital market since 1929 has been distorted by unusual developments. The crash then was such a horrifying experience for investors that for two whole decades thereafter, common stocks were regarded with great skepticism. This mistrust in the safety of common stock dividends served to keep stock prices much lower and yields much higher than normal.

Concurrently, during the 1930s and 1940s, the government's easy-money policies forced interest rates—and, hence, bond yields—to drop sharply. Thus, for about twenty years, bond yields were artificially depressed by Washington.

After World War II, conditions in these two key investment markets gradually returned to normal, and stock and bond yields began to seek their own levels. But as can be seen in the chart, it wasn't until the mid-1950s that stock and bond yields finally returned to the relationship that had prevailed throughout the first thirty years of the twentieth century. But even then, bond yields were lower

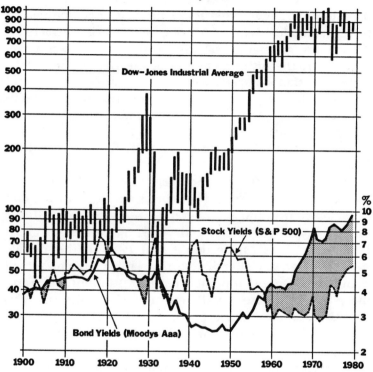

Still Overpriced

Dow–Jones Industrial Average

Stock Yields (S&P 500)

Bond Yields (Moodys Aaa)

In a freely competitive market, common stocks must compete with other investment vehicles for long-term capital. A comparison of stock yields with bond yields is therefore one way to evaluate equities. For two decades now, stocks have offered conspicuously less current income to investors than bonds. This is a main reason for the market's lackluster performance in the 1970s. Until stock yields approximate bond yields, equities must still be recognized as overpriced.

than the levels typical of the first three decades. Believing that bond yields would move still higher (and bond prices lower), institutional portfolio managers began putting more and more new money into equities instead.

Moreover, after stocks finally started recovering from their unusually depressed levels in 1950, they doubled in price in just five years. This phenomenal rise attracted a brand new generation of investors—one that was unrestrained by the bitter memories of the Depression. Thus, a combination of speculative and institutional demand extended the long bull market in stocks into the late 1960s even though, by most traditional standards, the majority of issues had already been overvalued for a decade. Result: stocks were acutely overpriced; stock yields were ridiculously low.

In the 1970s the gap between bond yields and stock yields started to narrow. That corresponded with the end of the postwar bull market. Even so, the correction still has a long way to go, since bond yields have risen so much lately. But there's little doubt that later in this decade stocks will at last offer investors a larger current return than bonds. Once that point is reached, I submit, more and more private investors will return to the equity market. And that's when the next primary bull market will begin. You can then start investing in stocks heavily and confidently.

One more point: for a long time now, pretax corporate earnings have been subjected to double taxation. The corporation first has to pay corporate income taxes. Then when it distributes part of its after-tax earnings to shareholders, the latter must pay taxes on the dividend income. If Congress sees fit to correct this unfair situation and remove dividend taxes, the attraction of equities would be significantly enhanced. And a new bull market could well emerge immediately thereafter as a result.

CHAPTER EIGHTEEN

Defense and Aerospace

Regardless of what happens to the general economy, the defense and aerospace industries will almost surely show significant growth in the 1980s. This will afford investors an opportunity to make commitments—*during periods when the market is especially weak*—in selected stocks that offer superior long-term capital growth potentials.

The figures tell the story. At present, the Soviet Union has approximately 6,500 nuclear weapons in its strategic arsenal. Even if Moscow adheres to the terms of Salt II, the number is expected to exceed 9,500 by 1985. And if the Russians deploy a new ICBM with ten reentry vehicles, as permitted by the proposed Salt II agreement, they would end up with an estimated 12,500 nuclear warheads by 1990.

Meanwhile, the Soviets have built hundreds of fortified command posts and have developed the kind of command control and communications systems capable of waging a full-scale nuclear war. They have also erected a formidable defense network that includes more than 6,000 radar stations, 2,600 interceptor aircraft, and 12,000 surface-to-air missiles.

For years, Washington ignored this Soviet arms buildup. A variety of special interest groups insisted that the government put increasing emphasis on social spending, cutting defense expenditures in the process. As a result, the U.S. armed forces are not only short of strategic weapons, they lack conventional equipment as well.

To counter the Soviet buildup in nuclear weapons and strategic defenses, the United States at last launched several major programs toward the end of the 1970s. These programs, together with a strengthening of conventional forces, will require a sharp boost in defense spending during the 1980s. These plans are based on the assumption that the Russians will adhere to the terms of the unratified Salt II. Should the Soviets decide to ignore the agreement, which is quite likely, they could well increase the number of nuclear warheads in their arsenal to about 21,000 by the end of the decade. The U.S. must then do still more to catch up.

Partly for this reason, the Pentagon has been formulating a new nuclear policy. Whereas the United States had long relied on its ability to destroy Russian cities and industrial complexes as a deterrent to a major conflict, it is now implementing a much broader strategy that includes hitting Russia's military targets and achieving the ability to wage a protracted war.

This means that programs for modernizing our strategic forces will have to be further accelerated, efforts to develop a new generation of guided missiles will have to be stepped up, and research relating to space and advanced weapon systems will have to be intensified.

Because of the additional outlays involved, defense spending as a percent of the GNP could rise from 4.59% in 1979 to 6.0–6.5% by 1982 or 1983. The ratio would re-

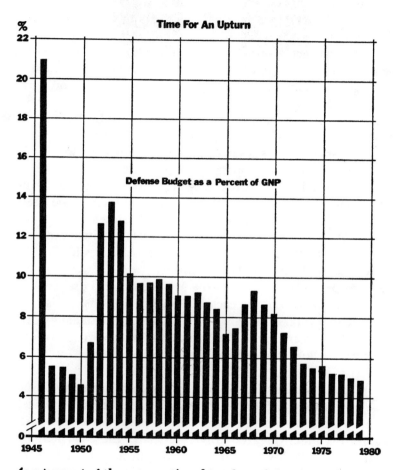

Time For An Upturn

Defense Budget as a Percent of GNP

As a percent of the gross national product, defense spending in 1979 was the lowest in nearly thirty years. With the Reagan administration emphasizing "peace through strength," a dramatic reversal of the downward trend can be confidently anticipated for the years ahead.

main below the 7%–9% range which prevailed even prior to the Vietnam War. Even so, the defense and aerospace industries could achieve a growth rate well in excess of 20% a year; many individual defense companies would do even better.

As matters now stand—that is, even without the increases to be recommended by the Reagan administration—the government plans to spend over $100 billion on strategic weapons alone during the first half of the 1980s. The Department of Defense, for example, has budgeted for land-based ICBMs over $30 billion, one-third of which will be spent on research and development and two-thirds on procurement and construction of launching sites.

Projects include the upgrading of the Titan and Minuteman missiles. But the bulk of the money will be used for the development of the MX mobile system. This program is being given top priority because the increased accuracy of Soviet missiles has rendered U.S. missile silos located at fixed sites highly vulnerable.

As presently conceived, the MX system will use twenty-three shelters to house each of 200 MX ICBMs. This will result in a total of 4,600 shelters, making it extremely difficult for the enemy to determine the exact location of the missiles at any given time, and extremely costly for them to try to attack all possible launch sites.

The missile itself will have nearly four times the throw weight of the Minuteman III missile. Moreover, technical improvements and the use of high-grade propellants will give it a much greater range. Initially, the MX will be capable of deploying ten warheads; an advanced reentry vehicle could result in a larger payload later on.

Site preparation will get under way in 1982, and full-scale shelter construction is scheduled to begin in 1984. *Thiokol, General Tire, Hercules,* and *Rockwell* will produce the various stages of the missile. And *Boeing* will be responsible for transport vehicles and related ground-support equipment.

The Department of Defense has also budgeted $12.4 billion for air-based strategic weapons over the next five years. Of this amount, $3.3 billion will be spent on research and development and $9.1 billion on procurement.

A major program involves the equipping of 151 B-52G bombers with air-launched cruise missiles. Unlike other weapons, the cruise force can function as unmanned aircraft and is, therefore, more capable of reaching designated targets. In fact, because the missiles can cruise in the air and then land for refueling, they can be launched on warning (pending assessment of the situation) or serve as a potent second-strike force.

Since each bomber will carry twenty ALCMs, more than 3,000 nuclear-armed missiles will be required for the program. Initial capability is scheduled for 1982 and full capability for 1990. The cost of the program is estimated at $4 billion. *Boeing* is the prime contractor for the air-launched cruise missile, but several other companies will share in the program.

Meanwhile, the Department of Defense plans to retain the remainder of the bomber force—ninety B-52Hs, seventy-five B-52Ds, and sixty FB-111s—as penetrating bombers. It believes that a mixed force of cruise missiles and penetrating bombers will pose the greatest challenge to Soviet air defense.

Unfortunately, without improved avionics, it may be difficult for the B-52 bombers to penetrate Soviet defenses a few years hence. But this will be compensated for by the procurement of 155 stretched FB-111B/C bombers, which will significantly enhance our retaliatory capability in the meantime. The stretched FB-111B/C will carry three times the payload of the basic aircraft. Moreover, its speed at low altitudes is twice that of the B-52, and, flying at low altitudes, it is detectable in only a fraction of the radar sector. This should make it an effective low-level penetrating bomber, particularly since the Soviets are lagging in look-down, shoot-down radar technology.

The FB-111B/C program will cost an estimated $6.2 billion, with the first aircraft being delivered in 1983. Full operational capability is expected by 1986. *General Dynamics* will be the prime contractor.

Some consideration is also being given to restarting the B-1 program. But there are serious questions as to whether this aircraft would be capable of penetrating Soviet air defenses. Moreover, many feel that the program would not be cost effective, particularly if the B-1 were limited to acting as a platform for air-launched cruise missiles.

As a result, efforts are being made to develop an entirely new long-range bomber to meet the needs of the 1990s. Such an aircraft would probably be tailored for low-level penetrating missions. Moreover, it would have to have extremely low radar and infrared signatures in order to escape enemy detection.

Some prototypes of the so-called stealth aircraft are already being tested. These utilize materials and coatings which can absorb enemy radar waves, provide shields for engine exhausts to prevent detection by infrared sensors, and make use of unusual wing configurations to confuse enemy radar. But despite recent publicity, considerable development remains to be done. As a result, the stealth aircraft won't become a reality until the end of the decade. *Boeing, Lockheed,* and *Rockwell* are among those companies working in this area.

Finally, the Department of Defense has budgeted $24.3 billion for sea-based strategic weapons over the next five years. The bulk of the money will be used to add fourteen Trident submarines to the fleet. Each vessel will carry twenty-four ballistic missiles with the capacity to deliver multiple warheads. As a result, the payload of just one Trident submarine will equal that of the ten Polaris submarines currently deployed in the Pacific.

The Trident I missile will have a range of 4,000 nautical miles, compared to 2,500 nautical miles for the Poseidon C-3 missile. And the Trident II, now under development, will extend the range to nearly 6,000 nautical miles.

Since there are 11 million square miles in the Pacific and 5.5 million in the Atlantic, the increased range will make it easier for the Trident submarine to hide and survive during a nuclear war. Moreover, thanks to its extended range, the Trident will be able to operate from stations on the East and West Coasts of the United States; it will not have to depend on foreign bases.

The first Trident submarine will be commissioned in 1981, and the remaining thirteen are expected to be authorized by 1986. *General Dynamics* will build the submarines, while *Lockheed* is the prime contractor for the Trident missile.

Needless to say, the deployment of the MX, cruise, and Trident missiles will help the United States in maintaining nuclear parity with the Soviet Union. But to strengthen the nation's overall strategic posture, the Department of Defense will also spend several billion dollars to modernize its command control and communications network. This is especially important in view of the fact that the new nuclear strategy requires an ability to wage a protracted war.

The keystone of the nation's command control and communications system is its early warning network. This has been expanded over the years to include space satellites, and efforts are currently under way to upgrade various ground facilities. In the case of an ICBM attack, the network is able to give our military leaders thirty minutes in which to respond. And the development of over-the-horizon radar is expected to provide similar warning against low-flying bombers.

Unfortunately, an increase in the number of Soviet ballistic missile submarines off the East Coast has cut the response time to twelve minutes as far as Washington is concerned. As a result, top priority is being given to a program that will increase the government's ability to direct our military forces from airborne command posts capable of surviving the first phase of a nuclear exchange.

The program will use the new *Boeing* E-4B aircraft and converted E-4As equipped with highly sophisticated monitoring and communications devices. In addition to a central command post, the system will have two auxiliary command posts; three control aircraft capable of launching Minuteman missiles; and two radio relay aircraft. Communication will be maintained with the fleet of eight airborne command aircraft kept on continuous alert by Strategic Air Command.

Another important project is the extremely low frequency (ELF) communications system that will be used by the Trident submarine fleet. The ELF system, which will become operational in 1985, will free the submarines from being tethered to an antenna on or near the surface. This means that the submarines will be able to utilize the ocean depths more effectively in order to escape detection. And since the ELF system can relay messages from either ground or airborne command posts, it will greatly increase the ability of the Trident fleet to function during a protracted war.

Besides long-range strategic weapons and defense, plans are also under way to modernize tactical nuclear forces in Europe. At present, the Warsaw Pact nations have a total of 1,370 medium-range systems in operation, compared to only 386 for NATO. These systems include ground-launched ballistic missiles, sea-launched ballistic missiles, medium-range bombers, and heavy fighter-bombers. To make matters worse, the Warsaw Pact is expected to add about fifty ballistic missiles and thirty Backfire bombers to its forces each year during the coming years.

As a countermeasure, beginning in 1983 NATO plans to deploy 464 ground-launched cruise missiles produced by *General Dynamics* and 108 mobile Pershing 2 missiles produced by *Martin Marietta*. This will help to restore the nuclear balance in Europe. But more important, because the cruise and Pershing 2 missiles will have the capacity to reach targets in the USSR, they could act as a major deterrent to nuclear war.

Meanwhile, the United States is taking steps to beef up its conventional forces. Among the major aircraft programs, for example, is the *General Dynamics* F-16 multimission fighter. Approximately 1,400 will be procured by the Air Force, and another 400 will be used by NATO forces. Production of the single-engine fighter is in the early stages.

Equally important is the *McDonnell Douglas–Northrop* F/A-18 multimission strike fighter, which will replace the F-4 and A-7 aircraft. The Navy and Marine Corps plan to buy 1,377 F/A-18s over the next five years at an estimated cost of $29 billion.

And a new fighter (designated the FX) is being developed for export. This aircraft will primarily fulfill a defense role. Delivery could begin as early as 1983, with sales totaling several billion dollars.

At the same time, the United States has finally started production of the XM-1 main battle tank. This vehicle, which will be produced by *Chrysler,* has nearly twice the speed of tanks currently in operation and much better maneuverability. In addition, it incorporates a number of improvements in fire control, fire power, and armor protection. The Army is expected to purchase about 7,000 XM-1s in the 1980s at a cost of nearly $10 billion.

The government also plans to spend $9 billion over the next five years to create a Rapid Deployment Force. Most of the money will be used to develop a new transport aircraft capable of carrying tanks and other heavy equipment. The aircraft (dubbed the CX) will make it possible for the United States to respond quickly to threats in any part of the world. As presently envisioned, the CX fleet will consist of fifty aircraft. But the figure is likely to double by the end of the decade. Companies in a good position to get the CX contract are *McDonnell Douglas, Lockheed,* and *Boeing.*

In addition, the Navy will spend about $1.5 billion to procure fifteen cargo vessels. These ships will be loaded with equipment and other military supplies and prepositioned at strategic locations around the world. This way, the United States will be able to react on very short notice.

When it comes to conventional warfare, however, the USSR is able to field a much larger force than the United States. Moreover, the buildup of Soviet ships, aircraft, and tanks in recent years has put this country at a severe disadvantage.

To redress the imbalance, the U.S. must develop entirely new weapons systems based on advanced technology. This is almost certain to lead to a new generation of tactical missiles by the late 1980s, which could drastically change the way in which conventional war is fought.

Actually, major improvements are already being made on existing systems such as the Sidewinder and Sparrow air-to-air missiles and the Maverick air-to-ground missile. And several other weapons will be added to the inventory over the next few years, including the Patriot and Roland ground air-defense missiles and the Hellfire antitank missile. Most of these systems will use infrared or millimeter-wave target seekers, greatly improving their effectiveness under all weather conditions.

But the big breakthrough will come from the use of large-scale integrated circuitry and minicomputers, which will increase the sensory and signal-processing capacity of the missiles several thousand times. This will permit the missiles to see complete targets, virtually eliminating the possibility that they will zero in on the wrong target or be fooled by decoys. In addition, they will be programmed to choose between several targets after launch, making it possible for them to adapt to changing battlefield conditions. And because of the improved sensory and signal-processing capability, they will be able to take evasive action to avoid enemy countermeasures.

Since a new generation of "fire and forget" missiles would have the potential for neutralizing superior forces, efforts to develop such weapons are expected to accelerate over the next few years. Moreover, because it costs much less to produce a missile than it does to produce a tank or other piece of heavy equipment, a much larger portion of the defense budget is likely to be allocated to such weapons in the future. *Hughes* and *Raytheon* are among the companies which could benefit from the development of such weapons.

Finally, it should be emphasized that space operations are becoming a part of many military systems, and will grow in importance during the 1980s. In fact, the United States already depends to a large extent on satellites and other space systems for early warning, navigation, reconnaissance, and electronic intelligence. And an estimated 70% of Defense Department communications are now being routed through space.

The Soviets, too, are aware of the military importance of space. In the past decade, they have conducted more than three times as many space launches as the United States. Their manned space program continues to receive top priority. And they have already developed a high-energy laser weapon capable of destroying satellites in low orbit.

As a result, the United States is expected to step up its space program over the next few years. A major task will be to develop systems that can operate from fortified satellites not vulnerable to enemy attacks. Such systems will provide early warning and bomber attack assessment. Moreover, their infrared sensors produce a high-resolution mosaic image much more informative than sensors provided in the past. At the same time, the launching of a data system satellite will provide two-way transpolar communications capable of operating in spite of electronic jamming.

In addition, the United States is expected to deploy high-energy laser weapons in space. Initially, these will be used to defend satellites and other space systems. But over the longer term, such weapons could conceivably be used to intercept hostile ICBMs in space before they can reach their targets in the United States. Such a development is probably at least ten years off. But by mid-decade, the U.S. could be in a position to use laser weapons aboard high-flying aircraft to guard against submarine-launched missiles. Some of the companies involved in high-powered lasers and antisatellite weapons are *TRW, General Electric, United Technology, AVCO,* and *Perkin-Elmer.* In addition, the *Rockwell* Navstar global positioning system will have an important role to play in space communications.

From the foregoing, it can be seen that a large number of companies will benefit from a higher level of defense spending. The MX, cruise, and Trident missile programs will account for a major portion of the increase during the early part of the decade, but tactical missiles and space weapons will have a much more important role to play by the late 1980s.

According to the latest figures, the ten largest defense contractors in order of rank are: *General Dynamics, Mc-Donnell Douglas, United Technology, Lockheed, General Electric, Litton, Boeing, Hughes, Raytheon,* and *Grumman.*

Other important contractors not mentioned previously include *Textron, Sperry Rand, RCA, Honeywell, Westinghouse, Fairchild Industries, LTV,* and *FMC.* In addition, several smaller companies that manufacture support systems or supply components stand to benefit from a boost in defense procurement.

CHAPTER NINETEEN

New Growth Areas

Besides defense and aerospace, there are a few other industries that promise to show handsome growth in the 1980s even though the general economic prospects are less than bright. Investments in these areas should prove rewarding—provided they are made during periods of market weakness when mass selling has brought their prices down from their current overpriced levels.

Coal. The coal industry, as I noted in Chapter 7, will show significant growth in the 1980s. Domestic production is expected to increase from 815 million tons a year in 1980 to 1.2 billion tons by the end of the decade. This translates into an average annual growth rate of 4.7%, which would be roughly twice what I foresee for the real GNP.

Foreign demand will be an important factor. In the past, exports to Western Europe and elsewhere have accounted for 8%–10% of U.S. production. But because of the higher OPEC prices and a cutback in the amount of coal available from Eastern Europe, the figure will probably rise to 12.5% by 1990. This would result in exports of 150 million tons a year, some 75% above the current level.

But that's only part of the story. By the mid-1980s, improved methods of burning coal are expected to reduce pollution problems and result in a much more favorable cost structure. This will encourage many industrial and utility companies in the U.S. to switch to coal or to specify coal for new facilities.

When this happens, a surge in domestic consumption will combine with a strong export market to create boom conditions within the industry. And a number of stocks should prove to be excellent vehicles for capital gains.

At present, electric utility companies account for 75% of U.S. coal consumption. Some 273 coal-fired generating plants are scheduled to come onstream by 1990, and the Department of Energy has targeted another 107 plants for conversion. All told, this will boost domestic demand by about 350 million tons.

Industrial companies will also increase their consumption. Cement producers, for instance, have already converted 80% of their plants to coal. And several other industries are expected to follow suit as the product becomes more economical to use.

On the basis of fuel costs, coal already has a big advantage over oil and gas. In mid-1980, for example, the delivered price of coal to electric utility plants averaged $1.34 per million BTUs, well below the $3.95 for oil and $2.04 for gas.

But corporate planners must include capital costs in their budgets. The fact is, combustion equipment used for coal is much more bulky and expensive than that used for oil or gas. And the installation of scrubbers and other devices to meet clean air standards can further increase the capital costs by as much as 40%. For this reason, many industrial and utility companies have delayed switching over to coal in recent years. As world oil prices keep climbing, however, the switchover is likely to accelerate.

The development of technology for fluidized bed combustion should help. In the atmospheric version, to be specific, coal is burned in a fluidized bed of inert ash and limestone. This not only inhibits the formation of nitrogen oxide, but also makes it possible to remove sulfur from the coal while it is still in the combustion chamber. In short, the technology results in considerable savings and makes it possible to use cheaper, high-sulfur coal, as well.

The pressurized version, which will become available in the mid-1980s, is similar to the atmospheric system except that the coal and bed material are injected into a pressurized combustion chamber. When this technology is combined with steam and gas turbines to produce electricity, plant efficiency can be increased 10%–20%.

Because of lead times in planning and construction, the switch to coal will probably require several years. But considerable momentum is expected to be generated by the middle of the decade, and should carry over into the 1990s.

Several coal companies will benefit from the increase in consumption, including the Consolidated Coal subsidiary of *Conoco, North American Coal, Pittston,* and *Westmoreland.* In addition, a number of coal-carrying railroads will participate in the industry's growth, as will the manufacturers of mining and combustion equipment.

Synfuels. Over the long term, an increasing amount of coal will be used as feedstock for chemicals and for the production of synthetic fuels. Current projections indicate that the synfuel industry will be capable of producing 1.5 million barrels/day by the late 1980s and 5 million barrels/day in the 1990s.

Gas and liquids derived from coal will account for about half of the total synfuel production. SASOL, Ltd. in South Africa is already producing large quantities of such synfuel. If SASOL-type plants were used in this country, it would require an investment of $155 billion to meet the target set for the 1990s. Because of the heavy financing involved, it will probably take time to get some projects off the ground. Shortages of engineers and equipment could also produce delays during the early stages of construction.

By the late 1980s, however, these problems should be overcome. And the introduction of second generation synfuel plants will help to increase operating efficiency and reduce production costs. Thus, most synfuel facilities using coal are expected to be profitable once they have gone through a shakedown period.

Oil shale will account for the remaining synfuel production. If land owned by the federal government is utilized, an investment of about $150 billion will be required to meet the goal set for the 1990s. Admittedly, the financing of projects and environmental considerations will cause some problems here also in the early 1980s. But they are likely to fade once the technology proves itself.

In fact, several surface processes have already been developed and operated on a small scale. When commercial plants are built, it should be possible to show rapid improvement in technology and efficiency. The use of fluidized beds, for example, would substantially reduce the cost of heating the crushed shale rock to produce oil and other products. Several of the major oil companies and a number of utility companies are involved in coal gasification projects. *Occidental Petroleum* and *Tosco* are among the leaders in oil and shale technology.

Gasohol. In the meantime, the nation is expected to reduce its dependence on foreign oil by boosting its consumption of gasohol. In the summer of 1979, I predicted that one-tenth of the country would switch to gasohol within a period of a few years. This would require 1.1 billion gallons of ethanol (grain alcohol) and result in a $2 billion market at current prices.

Subsequently, the government set a goal of increasing ethanol production from 80 million gallons a year to 500 million gallons by the end of 1981. This is in line with my forecast, and recent announcements by ethanol producers indicate that my target will be met by mid-1982.

Basically, gasohol is a mixture of unleaded gasoline and 200-proof ethanol. The two components are mixed in proportions of 90% gasoline and 10% alcohol. Significantly, ethanol is distilled from corn and other agricultural products. Thus, unlike petroleum, it can be "grown" year after year.

In those states allowing a tax credit, the price of gasohol is comparable to that of unleaded premium. Most motorists are willing to pay a higher price because they get better mileage with gasohol. Besides, the product usually results in lower maintenance costs and longer engine life.

Since one bushel of corn yields 2½ gallons of ethanol, it would take about 6% of our annual corn crop to produce 1.1 billion gallons of alcohol. If the entire nation were to switch over to gasohol, say by the end of the decade, it would take a little over half the U.S. corn crop.

Some critics have argued that this would have a devastating effect on our food supply. But in wet corn milling, all the nutrients are removed at the beginning of the grinding process. The remaining starch is then converted into sugar or alcohol. Thus, the only impact of gasohol would be to reduce the supply of sugar, which is already too large a part of the American diet.

Note that most projections related to gasohol are based on existing technology. But by using an improved strain of yeast, one company has already been able to increase efficiency in converting sugar to alcohol by 25%. This has made it possible to produce the same amount of alcohol with 20% less corn.

Further improvements in converting corn-based sugar to alcohol are expected to stretch the supply even more. And by the mid-1980s, it should become economical to use other agricultural products for the production of ethanol.

Meanwhile, production costs will show a significant decline. For one thing, increased efficiency in converting sugar to alcohol will bring about a sizable reduction in raw material costs. For another, by switching to a continuous process, producers will be able to cut fermentation time from between fifty and seventy hours to a little over twenty hours. Thus, there will be considerable savings in labor and overhead expenses.

Altogether, we estimate improved technology will reduce the cost of producing ethanol by 30%–35%. When this happens, gasohol should become much more competitive with gasoline. *Archer Daniels, CPC International, National Distillers, Publicker,* and *Staley* are among the ethanol producers most likely to benefit from the industry's growth.

The prospects for the 1990s are even brighter. By then, methanol (wood alcohol) is expected to play an important role as a fuel. In fact, research in this area is intensifying because agricultural and forest residues have the potential for meeting a large part of our energy requirements.

The production of methanol from organic material is

similar to the production of ethanol. The main difference is that, before converting the sugar into alcohol, it is necessary to break down the cellulose in the material being used. The first step is to treat the material with dilute sulfuric acid. This is followed by the use of special enzymes, which hydrolyze the cellulose into glucose, a simple form of sugar.

Because methanol can be made from corn cobs, wood chips, and other waste products, the technology can produce substantial savings in raw material costs. One company is already planning to build a plant that will have the capacity for converting wood chips into 100 million gallons of methanol a year. And other facilities are expected to come onstream by the middle of the decade.

The amount of methanol that can be used in gasohol is presently limited to 3%. But by modifying automobile engines, the percentage could be increased several times over. The product is expected to be used extensively as a boiler fuel, particularly in industrial applications.

As a result, methanol will probably become an important source of energy starting in the late 1980s. Together with ethanol, it should go a long way toward reducing our dependence on foreign oil.

Genetic Engineering. Scientists are now able to take a gene from one organism and combine it with the genetic material of another. When this is done, bacteria can be used as miniature factories to mass produce hormones, enzymes, and other natural substances. And because bacteria replicate so rapidly, substances can be produced much more economically than with conventional methods.

The first wave of recombinant DNA products will be in the health care area. Scientists are already producing insulin and growth hormones. And more recently, they have learned how to produce interferon, a natural substance that is effective against viruses and certain forms of cancer.

Recombinant DNA will also be used to produce vaccines and to develop antibiotics that are more potent, but have fewer side effects than products available today. In addition, the technique should eventually lead to the cloning of antibodies that can be used to fight a wide variety of infectious diseases.

Such products as these involve billion-dollar markets. But genetic engineering will also have an important role to play in medical diagnosis. Many clinical tests today are based on measuring different types of protein. Researchers, however, are working on a new technique that "fingerprints" DNA in order to diagnose specific problems.

One company using this technique has already developed a test for hepatitis and is in the process of developing another for sickle cell anemia. Over the longer term, it should be possible to develop other tests for detecting cancer. Significantly, the results of such tests can be made available within twenty-four hours, instead of the usual three to four days.

The second wave of DNA products will be in the agricultural area. Researchers are already working on improved strains of yeast that will make it more economical to produce gasohol. And they are trying to develop new kinds of bacteria that can be used to convert organic material to methanol.

Meanwhile, food processors have started to use recombinant DNA in an effort to modify the characteristics of certain basic commodities. One processor, for example, is trying to develop a strain of soybeans that will have an improved taste. This would broaden the market for soy protein as a meat substitute and help consumers to save on food costs. Another processor is trying to develop a new kind of peanut that would be tasty, but have a lower fat content. In this case, the product would fill an important segment in the low-calorie market.

The biggest effort in the agricultural area, however, will be directed toward developing hybrid grains capable of fixing nitrogen. This would be accomplished by combining nitrogen-fixing genes from legumes with wheat and other types of grain. If successful, the hybrid varieties would greatly reduce the need for fertilizer, saving farmers millions of dollars a year.

The third wave of DNA products will be in the industrial area. Researchers have already developed microbial methods for leaching minerals from low-grade ores. Further improvements resulting from recombinant DNA could lead to a substantial reduction in mining costs, while extending the life of proven reserves.

Genetic engineers may also be capable of developing new forms of bacteria which can be used to degrade pollutants and toxic wastes. If so, the technology could help the nation to solve many of its environmental problems at a reasonable cost.

Finally, by the late 1990s, genetic engineers are expected to develop biotechnical systems to replace catalytic processes in petroleum refining and the production of specialty chemicals. Such systems would have the potential for stretching our energy supplies. Eventually, they could make it more economical to convert coal into gas and other useful products.

Admittedly, some of the claims being made for genetic engineering may seem farfetched. After all, we are talking about markets that involve billions and billions of dollars. But DNA should be viewed primarily as an *information system* which can be manipulated to achieve specific results in the health care, agricultural, and industrial fields. Within this context, the possibilities appear immense.

Until recently, most of the advances in genetic engineering have come from a handful of small research companies. These include *Bethesda Research Laboratories, Biogen, Cetus, Genentech,* and *Genex.* But major drug companies such as *Abbot, Lilly, Merck, Schering-Pough,* and *Upjohn* will also have an important role to play. And over the longer term, several industrial companies will be active participants, including *DuPont, General Electric, INCO, Lubrizol, Monsanto, Standard Oil of California,* and *Standard Oil of Indiana.*

Videodiscs. Videodiscs represent another area that will show excellent growth in the 1980s. Current projections are that annual sales of disc players will exceed 5 million by the end of the decade. And sales of prerecorded discs are expected to be in the range of 200 million to 250 million. All told, this would result in a $7.5 billion market.

At present, three different systems are available. The one developed by RCA uses a microscopic diamond-tipped stylus and provides an hour's worth of programs on each side of the disc. The player sells for about $500 and the accompanying discs at $15 to $25, less than half the price of prerecorded videotapes. As output increases, these prices are likely to decline. Because of its relatively low cost, the RCA system will probably capture a large portion of the commercial market.

The system developed by N. V. Philips uses a laser to read pits pressed into a silvery disc. It sells for $775. However, unlike the RCA system, it can page through all 54,000 frames on one side of a disc or display any single frame randomly. As a result, the player is likely to capture most of the industrial market.

A third system developed by the JVC subsidiary of Matsushita represents a compromise between the other two systems. It sells for about $650, but includes some of the features found on the Philips machine.

Unfortunately, the three systems are not compatible; none will play discs manufactured for the other machines. This could lead to some confusion over the next couple of years. Nevertheless, the videodisc market is expected to show rapid growth, with each system carving out an important niche for itself.

The commercial or home market will be the first to develop. In the early years, movies are likely to be the most popular item. But music programming will become more significant as new art forms and formats are devised to take advantage of the medium. In addition, videodiscs will be used extensively for home instruction in a wide variety of subjects such as tennis, dancing, and guitar playing.

The industrial market will be the next to develop. Initially, videodiscs will be used for sales presentations, training programs, and the like. But because of the relatively low cost, they are expected to be used extensively in word processing and data storage. In fact, the product could hasten the day of the "electronic" office.

The educational market will probably be the last to develop. This is because it will take time to produce the necessary software. Over the long term, however, videodiscs are expected to have an important role to play in education, particularly in vocational training and in such areas as the life sciences and engineering, in which visual knowledge is part of the learning process.

The RCA system will utilize players made by *RCA* and *Zenith,* videodiscs manufactured by *RCA* and *CBS,* and program materials produced by *CBS* and *MGM.* The *Philips* system will utilize players made by that company's Magnavox subsidiary and *Pioneer Electronic,* discs manufactured by *Philips* and *IBM,* and program material produced by *MCA.* The JVC system will utilize hardware and software produced by *JVC, General Electric,* and *Thorn EMI.*

South Africa. Internationally minded investors may find South Africa of interest for the 1980s. At present, most Americans invest in South African shares through the purchase of American Depository Receipts, commonly known as ADRs. These are generally limited to gold mining companies. But over the next few years, we expect an active market to develop for ADRs in other areas, including manufacturing and construction.

Meanwhile, by using financial rands, Americans are able to purchase South African shares directly on the Johannesburg Exchange. Most large brokerage houses in the U.S. are equipped to handle such transactions, charging a small fee for the service.

South Africa is a country rich in natural resources. It has a well-developed free enterprise economy and enjoys relatively low labor cost. Until now, American investors focused their attention on gold shares to the exclusion of almost everything else. This is understandable, particularly in view of the sharp rise in gold prices since 1978.

What has gone unnoticed is the impact that higher gold prices are having on the South African economy. According to the latest budget, government revenues from gold mines will rise 65% in fiscal 1981. This in turn will permit an 11.3% reduction in personal income taxes, while at the same time strengthening the government's fiscal position.

The reduction in personal income taxes has already stimulated consumer spending by increasing disposable income. And the higher level of economic activity is expected to promote private capital investment and employment during the coming months. This means that the real gross domestic product (GDP) will probably grow at an annual rate of 5%–6% during much of the 1980s.

Admittedly, the South African policy of apartheid has made some Americans leery of investing in South African shares. But the situation has been much exaggerated by the liberal press. The fact is, the blacks in that country enjoy a much better life than their counterparts in neighboring African countries. Moreover, the South African government has, in fact, taken steps to improve black-white relations. Meanwhile, a rising level of employment, particularly among blacks, should tend to dampen political turmoil and hasten reform.

Thus, an improved political and social environment and an abundance of raw material and labor should combine to make South Africa one of the most attractive areas abroad for investment.

CHAPTER TWENTY

A Few Final Words

In this book, I have tried to present to you in a coherent manner the economic and investment climate you can reasonably expect in the decade of the 1980s, and how you can make your wealth grow therein. Admittedly, some of what I have said, especially as it pertains to the early part of the 1980s, is not particularly cheerful. But, then, successful investing must come from a realistic appraisal of what's in prospect, and not from sugar-coated forecasts or upbeat political promises.

In presenting my case, I have made every effort to substantiate my views with easy-to-understand logic and solid statistics. It has often been said that economic and market research is more an art than a science. Maybe so. But all too often, economists and market analysts have gone too far in relying strictly on personal feelings and in ignoring clear-cut evidence. I submit that only by logically interpreting reliable facts and analyzing actual developments can one artfully envision the most probable economic and investment environment ahead.

I cannot overemphasize the need for investors to think

things out carefully and logically. Even if you don't agree with every one of my assumptions, I think I have given you enough historical and current facts with which to draw your own conclusion as to what the economy and the market are likely to do in the years ahead.

Once you have a clear-cut picture in mind, you'll be able to implement a coherent investment program that befits that investment climate. More importantly, you'll have enough conviction in what you are doing not to be bothered by minor and short-term reverses. This is important. A lot of money has been lost in the market by investors who succumb to emotions and lose faith in their own judgment.

This is not to say that the scenario I've presented herein, or the modified scenario you envision, is unalterable. Not at all. But I have shown you step by step how I arrived at my conclusions and why certain investment strategies are most suitable. Should future events develop differently, all you have to do is to use the same logical and analytical procedure. Just a little fine tuning will put you back on the right track.

The views I have presented in this book are in most cases at odds with conventional wisdom. But believe me, I'm not trying to be different just to be different. It's a sad fact that conventional wisdom has become conspicuously inadequate of late. Even now, it refuses to face up to the fact that the national balance sheet is in terrible shape.

The fact that I'm in a minority position means that you will keep hearing and reading views from noted experts that directly challenge my position. But if you agree with my logic, don't let other opinions upset you. Remember, just before the 1929 crash, Establishment experts had all declared that there was nothing wrong with the economy or the stock market. Don't forget also that most spokesmen connected with government, the big banks, or major corporations have a vested interest in making only bullish projections. In other words, their forecasts are often made for public relations purposes. It wouldn't be too wise for you to stake your hard-earned money on them.

While it's not safe to rely on the Establishment's rose-colored forecasts, it is not much better to be intimidated by the alarmists, who have lately become more and more numerous and vocal. Here again, common sense should be able to help you differentiate the sincere analysts from the opportunists. If you hear someone warning paradoxically that the real estate market is about to collapse and that runaway inflation is just around the corner, stay away from him. Avoid also those who bad-mouthed gold years ago, but are enthusiastically recommending its purchase now. They obviously don't know what they are talking about.

Finally, I must repeat what I said at the outset of this book: do your homework. Through this book I have helped you anticipate the underlying economic and market tides. By keeping abreast of current economic, monetary, and political developments, you may be able to identify and take advantage of some of the important surface waves as well. An investment program that factors in these changes will be that much more rewarding. So, don't be afraid of the harder times to come. You can very well be one of the few who prosper in the sobering years ahead.

Index